# I Can't Believe It's Not Meat!

## Roger, Diana & Monty Kilburn

Book Publishing Company
Summertown, Tenn.

Cover photos and design:
 Borella & Company
Interior design: Warren Jefferson

ISBN 1-57067-088-9

Kilburn, Roger
  I can't believe it's not meat! / Roger Diana
& Monty Kilburn.
    p cm.
  ISBN 1-57067-088-9 (alk. paper)
  1. Textured soy proteins. 2. Meat substitutes.
I. Kilburn, Diana. II. Kilburn, Monty. III. Title.
  TX558.S7.K55 2000
  641.6′5655--dc21            99-059389

Calculations for the nutritional analyses in this book are based on the average number of servings listed with the recipes and the average amount of an ingredient if a range is called for. Calculations are rounded up to the nearest gram. If two options for an ingredient are listed, the first one is used. Not included are fat used for frying (unless the amount is specified in the recipe), optional ingredients, or serving suggestions.

## Special Thanks

We would like to thank the following people:

Family members Mary Ellen Kilburn, Becky Kilburn and David Kice, Beckham Kilburn, Jackson Kilburn, Beck and Eula Kilburn, Tom and Mary Haskell, Danny Haskell and family, Mike Haskell and family, and the Elliotts for participating as our guinea pigs.

Bob and Cynthia Holzapfel for their friendship and collaboration on projects and sporting events.

Ron Pickarski, Marie Oser, Jon Tiede, Katey McGill, Elmer Schettler, Deb Wycoff, Donna Badding-Fleener, Alan Peters, Sean O'Neal, Tom Steuby, and everyone else who has offered assistance and inspiration.

# Table of Contents

I was introduced to the soybean before soy was hip, long before the chic and trendy consumed veggie burgers at the local bistro. Yup, I knew all about how the soybean was one of the most versatile and useful things on the planet. After all, I grew up in the house of a man whose life revolved around crushing that little bean.

I learned of the soybean's power and prowess on the many Saturday mornings spent in my dad's offices at various processing plants. I was always intrigued by the noises, the smells, and most of all the little display bottles of the products the different factories produced. Proudly displayed in the entrance of every plant were the powders, flakes, bits, and chunks that could be made from the infamous soybean.

But, I mostly remember the bashing of the soybean in the '70s. Like the ugly duckling or the nerdy kid, the soybean was publicly humiliated. School burgers were the joke of many stand-up comedy routines and a memory worse than reality for most school children. But the soybean and many industry elders (like my father) now are having the last laugh.

## Health Benefits of Soy

Cancer, heart disease, osteoporosis, and other ailments are no laughing matter. We study and treat these diseases with the hope of eliminating or, at a minimum, delaying their onset. Research confirms that diet can have a positive effect on these and many other afflictions.

Some of the most exciting studies focus on the soybean and its effects on the human body. Soyfoods have been linked with reducing the risk of heart disease, lowering cholesterol and high blood pressure, preventing certain cancers, limiting the progression of osteoporosis, and diminishing the discomforts of menopause.

Many researchers are trying to isolate the component of the soybean that is linked to these health benefits. However, the majority of studies have used a variety of soyfoods and incorporated these into the diets of the subjects. One such soyfood is textured soy.

## What is textured soy?

One of the most versatile and satisfying foods produced from the soybean is textured soy. Textured soy now comes in a variety of shapes, textures, flavors, and colors. Its most useful function comes in replacing various cuts of meat, like ground beef, cubed chicken, beef chunks, etc. Textured soy has very little flavor, so it can easily take on the flavors from marinades, sauces, or other ingredients in recipes. This makes it easy to incorporate soy into a daily diet without eating the same thing over and over.

Textured soy begins with the whole soybean. The hull of the bean is removed and used for animal feed. The oil is also removed and becomes the source for margarine, cooking oil, salad dressings, and many other commonly used foods. The remaining portion of the soybean is soy flour.

Soy flour, which is about 50% protein and contains almost no oil or fat, looks very similar to any wheat flour. The next step is to send the soy flour through an extruder, a long tube where the soy flour is heated and pushed through a small opening. The extruder forces the soy flour out at high pressure, and because this pressure creates very high temperatures, it changes the texture of the flour. When you add water to it, it will be chewy like meat. This product is commonly known as textured soy flour or textured soy protein.

Another textured soy product is textured soy protein concentrate. The sugars are removed from the soy flour, and the resulting product is then texturized like textured soy flour. Textured soy protein concentrate is 70% percent protein, and because the sugars have been removed, it is more easily digested by many people. (The sugars in soyfoods are what give people gas.) Textured concentrate can now be found in a number of exciting new shapes and sizes, ranging from large "chicken breast"-style pieces, chopped "chicken" cubes, larger "chicken" tenders, and even "pork-style" strips perfect for barbecue.

## How to use it

Think of textured soy as just another source of protein. When people go to the grocery store and contemplate what they'll have for dinner, most of them will focus on the main dish. Should I have beef or chicken, maybe fish? With textured soy, you can have it all.

The various products we use in these recipes have meat or poultry counterparts. The ground beef-style textured soy is similar in appearance to ground beef, unflavored chunks are similar to chunks of chicken. The beef styles contain caramel color and have a darker shade than the uncolored styles.

Flavoring is another factor when

using textured soy. The types of textured soy we will use are unflavored. In fact, the only ingredient in these textured soy products is soy flour or soy protein concentrate (except for the beef styles which have caramel color). This is the most important thing to remember when it comes to preparing dishes with textured soy; the soy products themselves have only a subtle flavor. Textured soy provides texture and, of course, the health benefits of the soybean, but its flavor is very bland. That's where you come in.

Textured soy is dry and must be simmered in liquid to hydrate. This is similar to marinating, where you can impart a variety of flavors to foods by allowing them to soak up herbs and spices, soy sauce, oils or vinegars, or any of your favorite accompaniments. If you hydrate textured soy with a beef- or chicken-style broth, it will taste like beef or chicken. If you hydrate it in a teriyaki marinade, it will have a teriyaki flavor, etc.

So in the recipes that follow, we use a vegetarian chicken-flavored broth and a vegetarian beef-flavored broth to hyrdate the textured soy products. This provides a base flavor, and any additional ingredients you include will add to that flavor. If you are concerned about sodium, then just use less broth to hydrate. One thing to remember when hydrating textured soy products is they absorb thin or clear broths or sauces the best and will not absorb thick or cream sauces quickly and completely.

Once hydrated, textured soy will look like meat and may even scare away some vegetarians. It really will amaze the most cynical of people, especially when you stare down the first textured soy you buy and wonder how something that looks like grape nuts really can make a prize-winning chili!

And that leads to my best advice—when you look at textured soy for the first time, don't look at it like the ugly duckling or the nerdy kid, because textured soy is superior to beef and chicken in many ways. You can have your favorite dishes without the fat, without the cholesterol, and, in many cases, without the added calories you would get from including meat or poultry. So use this cookbook as a starting point, realizing that any recipe out there calling for meat can be altered to accommodate textured soy. Remember, it is through experimentation and adventure that all great recipes (and chefs) are created.

*Monty Kilburn*
*Knoxville, Tennessee*

## Basic Preparation Instructions for Textured Soy Protein

Combine 1 cup textured soy protein and 1 cup vegetarian broth or water in a medium saucepan. Bring to a boil, cover, and reduce the heat to simmer. Continue to cook for 10 to 15 minutes, or until tender. Any excess water can be drained.

## Basic Preparation Instructions for Textured Soy Protein Concentrate

Combine 1 cup textured soy protein concentrate and 1¼ cups vegetarian broth or water in a medium saucepan. Bring to a boil, cover, and reduce the heat to simmer. Continue to cook for 10 to 15 minutes, or until tender. Any excess water can be drained.

## Basic Preparation Instructions for Chiken Breasts

Combine 4 Chiken Breasts and 3 cups vegetarian broth or water in a medium saucepan. Bring to a boil, cover, and reduce the heat to simmer. Continue to cook for 35 to 40 minutes, or until tender. Excess water can be drained.

---

You can order all the varieties of textured soy products used in this book (and many of the special foods listed on page 8) from:

The Mail Order Catalog for Healthy Eating
P.O. Box 180
Summertown, TN 38483
1-800-695-2241

*or shop online at:*
www.healthy-eating.com

*Mail Order Sources*

# A Note about Unusual Ingredients

Most of the ingredients you'll encounter in this cookbook are available in any local supermarket, but a few might be easier to find in a natural foods store or through mail order sources. Here is some additional information on some of the more unusual ingredients in our recipes.

*Cajun seasoning:* A blend of ground pepper and zesty spices unique to Cajun cooking. Look for this in the spice section of your supermarket or natural foods store.

*Dried mushrooms:* Buying dried mushrooms will allow to you to enjoy many varities that are not available fresh in your area or are not in season. They are available in many natural foods stores. Reconstitute dried mushrooms by soaking them in boiling water for 15 minutes. You can drain the mushrooms and use the soaking liquid to flavor sauces and broths; strain it through a coffee filter or paper towel first to remove any grit or small particles.

*Harvest Direct Sausage Seasoning:* A special blend of spices and herbs for recreating that special sausage-style flavor. Available through the mail order source on page 7.

*Nondairy cheeses:* It is now possible to get a variety of dairy-style cheeses—from traditional American to Swiss, cheddar, mozzarella, and cream cheese—in the form of nondairy substitutes. Look for these in the dairy section of your supermarket or natural foods store.

*Soy Parmesan substitute:* Soyco makes a delicious casein-free, totally vegetarian substitute for grated Parmesan. It is available in some natural foods stores and through the mail order source on page 7.

*Vegetarian Worcestershire sauce:* Traditional Worcestershire sauce contains anchovies, but there are brands available in some natural foods stores that are completely vegetarian. Also check the mail order source on page 7.

*Wasabi:* Extremely hot and flavorful Japanese horseradish, best known to Americans as a dip for sushi. You can often find this in natural foods stores as a powder; reconstitute it by adding a small amount of water.

Unusual Ingredients

# I Can't Believe
# It's Not Meat!

# Appetizers

# Spinach Balls

*Yield: 8 servings*

*These smell so good as they are baking, the family will be salivating.*

1/2 cup water

1/2 cup unflavored textured soy protein granules

One 10-ounce package frozen spinach, cooked and drained

1 cup herbed stuffing mix

1/2 large onion, finely chopped

1/4 teaspoon chopped garlic

1 teaspoon Cajun seasoning or Harvest Direct Sausage Seasoning (see page 8)

1/8 teaspoon pepper

4 tablespoons dairy-free margarine, melted

In a small saucepan, bring the water to a boil. Add the textured soy granules, remove from the heat, and let stand 10 minutes.

Thoroughly mix the granules with the remaining ingredients in a mixing bowl, and let stand 15 minutes. Preheat the oven to 375°F. Firmly press the mixture into 1-inch balls, and arrange on a greased baking sheet. Bake for 25 minutes or until golden brown. Makes approximately 24.

Per Serving: Calories 97, Protein 5 g, Soy Protein 3 g, Fat 5 g, Carbohydrates 9 g, Sodium 294 mg

# Mexican Roll-Ups

Yield: 12 servings

*This is an easy appetizer to make ahead for parties.*

In a small saucepan, bring the water to a boil. Add the textured soy granules, broth powder, and salsa. Mix well and simmer for 2 minutes. Remove from the heat and let cool.

While preparing the filling, warm the tortillas either in the oven or microwave. Preheat the oven to 350°F. Wrap the tortillas in foil, and warm for 5 minutes. Or wrap 6 tortillas at at time in a cloth or paper towel that has been sprinkled with a little water. Microwave on high for about 30 to 45 seconds.

In a mixing bowl, blend the sour cream and cream cheese until smooth. Add the textured soy granules and remaining ingredients, and mix well. Spread the soy granule and cheese mixture on the warm tortillas, and roll up. Place seam side down in a glass baking dish. After filling all the tortillas, chill in the refrigerator until firm. Slice into half-inch sections, and serve. Makes 50 to 60.

¾ cup water

1 cup beef-style textured soy protein granules

2 teaspoons vegetarian beef-flavored broth powder or equivalent

¼ cup salsa

1 cup soy sour cream

8 ounces soy cream cheese

4 ounces canned green chile peppers, drained and chopped

6 ounces canned black olives, chopped (1 cup)

1 cup shredded low-fat non-dairy cheddar

3 chopped green onions

1 teaspoon garlic powder

12 flour tortillas

Appetizers

Per Serving: Calories 216, Protein 9 g, Soy Protein 6 g, Fat 10 g, Carbohydrates 22 g, Sodium 429 mg

# Sweet-n-Sour Samplers

*Yield: 8 servings*

*Increase the hot pepper sauce for a sweet-n-spicy dish.*

1 cup textured soy Chopped Chiken

1½ cups water

1 to 2 tablespoons vegetarian chicken-flavored broth powder or equivalent

1 cup peach jam or preserves

⅓ cup white wine vinegar

One 16-ounce can pineapple chunks, drained

1 garlic clove, minced

1 teaspoon hot pepper sauce

1 tablespoon soy sauce

1 red bell pepper, chopped

1 green bell pepper, chopped

Combine the Chopped Chiken, water, and broth powder in a medium saucepan. Bring to a boil, cover, and simmer for 15 minutes or until tender.

Add the remaining ingredients, and simmer for 15 to 20 minutes, or until the bell peppers are slightly tender. Serve with toothpicks as an appetizer or on rice as an entrée.

Appetizers

Per Serving: Calories 170, Protein 5 g, Soy Protein 5 g, Fat 0 g, Carbohydrates 37 g, Sodium 209 mg

# I Can't Believe It's Not Meat!

## Main Dishes

# Spicy Poultry-Style Burgers

*Yield: 5 servings*

*Fruit chutneys make a great topping for these zesty burgers.*

1 cup water

4 teaspoons chicken-flavored broth powder or equivalent

1 cup unflavored textured soy protein granules

1 tablespoon sesame seeds

1 green onion, finely chopped

1 large clove garlic, minced

½ tablespoon finely grated fresh gingerroot

1 tablespoon low-sodium soy sauce

¼ teaspoon pepper

½ teaspoon cayenne pepper

¼ cup whole-grain wheat flour

½ cup uncooked rolled oats

¼ cup canola oil

In a small saucepan, bring the water to a boil. Add the broth powder and textured soy granules. Mix thoroughly, remove from the heat, and let cool.

Toast the sesame seeds in a dry skillet. After the granules have cooled, combine all the ingredients, except the oil, in a large mixing bowl. Press together firmly into patties that are ¾-inch thick and about 3½-inches wide. In a large nonstick frying pan, heat the oil over medium-high heat, and cook the patties until browned on each side.

Main Dishes

Per Serving: Calories 220, Protein 11 g, Soy Protein 9 g, Fat 12 g, Carbohydrates 15 g, Sodium 323 mg

# Soy Barbecued Beans

*Yield: 8 servings*

*This can be thrown in a crockpot and cooked on low all day.*

In a small saucepan, bring the water to a boil. Add the textured soy granules and broth powder. Mix well and set aside for 10 minutes.

In a medium saucepan, heat the shortening. Add the onion, garlic, and bell pepper, and sauté over medium heat until the onion is tender. Add the textured soy granules and remaining ingredients, mix thoroughly, and cook for 5 minutes.

Preheat the oven to 350°F. Transfer the mixture to a 9 x 13-inch baking dish, and bake for 45 minutes to 1 hour.

¾ cup water

¾ cup beef-style textured soy protein granules

2 teaspoons vegetarian beef-flavored broth powder or equivalent

3 tablespoons oil

1 onion, chopped

1 clove garlic, chopped

1 small bell pepper, chopped

½ cup ketchup

½ cup sodium-free tomato juice

2 teaspoons chili powder

3 tablespoons anchovy-free Worcestershire sauce

1 teaspoon pepper

1 teaspoon celery seed

½ cup brown sugar

6 cups baked beans

Main Dishes

Per Serving: Calories 310, Protein 14 g, Soy Protein 4 g, Fat 1 g, Carbohydrates 59 g, Sodium 1129 mg

# Poultry-Style Divan

*Yield: 4 servings*

*Serve this dish with a wild rice pilaf.*

3 cups water

4 tablespoons vegetarian chicken-flavored broth powder or equivalent

1 cup unflavored textured soy protein granules

¼ cup dairy-free margarine

¼ cup all-purpose flour

½ cup nondairy milk

⅓ cup sherry

½ teaspoon pepper

Two 10-ounce packages frozen broccoli, cooked and drained

¼ cup soy Parmesan substitute

In a small saucepan, bring the water to a boil. Add the vegetarian chicken-flavored broth, and stir until mixed well. Set aside 2 cups of the broth in a small bowl. Add the textured soy granules to the remaining hot broth in the saucepan. Mix well, and set aside for 10 minutes.

Melt the margarine in a medium saucepan, and stir in the flour. Slowly add the remaining 2 cups of broth. Bring the mixture to a boil, then reduce to a simmer, stirring constantly until thick. Remove from the heat and add the granules, nondairy milk, sherry, and pepper.

Place the drained, cooked broccoli in a 9 x 13-inch baking dish. Pour the sauce over the broccoli, and sprinkle with the soy Parmesan. Broil for 5 minutes.

Main Dishes

Per Serving: Calories 274, Protein 21 g, Soy Protein 13 g, Fat 10.4 g, Carbohydrates 26 g, Sodium 855 mg

# Stuffed Tomatoes

*Yield: 6 servings*

*Any type of cooked greens pairs up nicely with this dish for a light meal.*

In a small saucepan, bring the water to a boil, add the broth powder, and mix well. Stir in the textured soy granules, and let cool.

Cut off the tops of the tomatoes, and scoop out the pulp. (Using a melon bailer or grapefruit spoon will make the job easier.) Chop the pulp, then drain off the resulting juice and set aside.

In a large nonstick skillet, melt the margarine over medium heat. Sauté the onion and green peppers about 5 to 7 minutes, then add the textured soy granules and sauté 2 minutes more. Add the chopped tomato pulp to the granule mixture, and stir in the corn syrup, Worcestershire sauce, basil, and pepper. Cook, stirring, for about 10 minutes until thick and bubbling. Remove from the heat, add the bread cubes and Parmesan, and mix well.

Preheat the oven to 350°F. Spoon the granule and vegetable mixture carefully into the tomato shells. Place the stuffed tomatoes into a baking dish large enough to hold all the tomatoes without crowding, and bake in the oven for 20 to 25 minutes. Top each tomato with 2 tablespoons shredded mozzarella, and continue baking for 5 minutes longer, or until the cheese is soft and bubbly.

- 1 cup water
- 4 teaspoons vegetarian beef-flavored broth powder or equivalent
- 1 cup beef-style textured soy protein granules
- 6 tomatoes
- 3 tablespoons dairy-free margarine
- ½ cup chopped onions
- ½ cup diced green peppers
- ¼ cup dark corn syrup
- 1 tablespoon anchovy-free Worcestershire sauce
- 1 teaspoon dried basil, or 2 teaspoons fresh basil
- ¼ teaspoon pepper
- 1 cup seasoned bread stuffing cubes
- ¼ cup soy Parmesan substitute
- ¾ cup shredded soy mozzarella

Per Serving: Calories 265, Protein 18 g, Soy Protein 12 g, Fat 8 g, Carbohydrates 38 g, Sodium 982 mg

Main Dishes

# Mom's Poultry-Style Stew & Dumplings

*Yield: 6 servings*

*One of the great comfort foods; serve with corn and green beans.*

4 cups water

4 teaspoons vegetarian chicken-flavored broth powder or equivalent

1 cup unflavored textured soy protein granules

3 carrots, sliced

2 yellow onions, chopped

2 teaspoons dried celery leaves

2 tablespoons dried parsley

½ teaspoon pepper

One 10 ¾-ounce can cream of mushroom soup (or 1 cup nondairy milk, 2 tablespoons cornstarch, and ½ cup diced mushrooms)

*Dumplings*

1⅔ cups biscuit mix

¼ teaspoon thyme

½ teaspoon pepper

1 tablespoon dried parsley

Egg replacer equivalent to 2 eggs

⅓ to ½ cup nondairy milk

In a stock pot, bring the 4 cups water to a boil. Add the broth powder and mix well, then stir in the textured soy granules, and reduce the heat to simmer. Add the carrots, onions, celery leaves, parsley, pepper, and cream of mushroom soup. Simmer over medium heat until the vegetables are tender.

In a mixing bowl, combine the biscuit mix, thyme, ½ teaspoon pepper, and 1 tablespoon dried parsley, and mix well. In a measuring cup, combine the egg replacer, ¼ cup water, and enough nondairy milk to make ⅔ cup total. Add the milk mixture to the dry ingredients, and mix well.

Using a teaspoon, drop the dumpling mixture into the simmering stew broth 1 teaspoon at a time. After adding the dumplings, cook 10 minutes over medium heat. Cover and continue cooking another 10 minutes.

NOTE: If you use nondairy milk instead of cream of mushroom soup, be sure to mix the cornstarch with the cold milk before adding it to the stock.

*Main Dishes*

Per Serving: Calories 263, Protein 13 g, Soy Protein 7 g, Fat 8 g, Carbohydrates 37 g, Sodium 765 mg

# Manicotti

*Yield: 7 servings*

*Children always love Italian food, so this recipe is always a big hit with youngsters.*

Cook the manicotti according to package instructions; drain and cool. In a small saucepan, bring the ¾ cup water to a boil. Add the broth powder and mix well, then add the soy granules. Let stand in a medium bowl for 10 minutes or until cool.

Combine the tofu, mozzarella, ¼ cup of the Parmesan, 2 tablespoons of the dried parsley, the herbs, pepper, and soy granules. Carefully stuff this mixture into the manicotti tubes.

Preheat the oven to 350°F. Arrange the filled manicotti in an oiled 9 x 13-inch baking dish. Cover with the spaghetti sauce, and sprinkle the remaining Parmesan and parsley over the top. Cover and bake for 20 minutes. Remove the cover and continue baking for 10 to 15 minutes, or until hot and bubbly.

NOTE: Using low-fat or non-fat cheeses will reduce the fat.

One 8-ounce package manicotti (about 14 tubes)

¾ cup water

2 teaspoons vegetarian beef-flavored broth powder or equivalent

¾ cup beef-style textured soy protein granules

2 cups mashed firm tofu

2 cups shredded soy mozzarella

½ cup soy Parmesan substitute

4 tablespoons dried parsley

1 teaspoon dried oregano

1 teaspoon dried basil

1 teaspoon pepper

One 32-ounce jar spaghetti sauce

Per Serving: Calories 443, Protein 28 g, Soy Protein 21 g, Fat 13 g, Carbohydrates 58 g, Sodium 1045 mg

Main Dishes

# Spaghetti Bolognese

*Yield: 10 servings*

*A great recipe to make ahead of time when having company.*

3 cups water

1¼ cups beef-style textured soy protein granules

4 tablespoons vegetarian beef-flavored broth powder or equivalent

2 tablespoons canola oil

3 cloves garlic, minced

5 ounces canned mushrooms, sliced

1 teaspoon dried parsley

¼ teaspoon basil leaves

½ teaspoon oregano

¼ teaspoon sage

2 tablespoons sweetener

One 28-ounce can stewed tomatoes

One 12-ounce can tomato paste

One 10¾-ounce can tomato puree

½ teaspoon anchovy-free Worcestershire Sauce

1 cup chopped onions

In a medium saucepan, bring the water to a boil. Add the textured soy granules and broth powder, mix well, and simmer for 10 minutes.

In a large stock pot, combine the remaining ingredients, and bring to a simmer. Add the textured soy mixture to the tomato mixture, and cook over low heat for 1½ hours. Serve over your favorite pasta.

Main Dishes

Per Serving: Calories 136, Protein 10 g, Soy Protein 5 g, Fat 4 g, Carbohydrates 25 g, Sodium 406 mg

# Texas Enchiladas

Yield: 6 servings

*Serve this spicy dish with rice and black beans.*

Mix the salsa, ¼ cup water, and broth powder in a small saucepan. Bring to a boil and add the textured soy granules. Remove from the heat and let cool. Mix the Monterey Jack, 1 cup cheddar, onion, sour cream, parsley, pepper, and cooled textured soy protein together. Set aside.

In a medium saucepan, make an enchilada sauce by heating the tomato sauce, ⅔ cup water, green pepper, chili powder, oregano, cumin, and garlic to boiling, stirring occasionally. Reduce the heat and simmer uncovered for 5 minutes. Pour into a 9-inch ungreased pie pan.

Preheat the oven to 350°F. Dip a tortilla into the enchilada sauce to coat both sides, and lay on a clean plate. Spoon on about ¼ cup of the textured soy mixture, and roll the tortilla around the filling. Arrange in an oiled 7 x 12-inch baking dish, and proceed with the remaining tortillas and filling mixture. Pour the remaining sauce over the enchiladas, and bake uncovered for about 15 minutes. Top with the ¼ cup shredded cheddar, and bake 5 more minutes, or until hot and bubbly.

1 cup salsa

¼ cup water

4 teaspoons vegetarian beef-flavored broth powder or equivalent

1 cup beef-style textured soy protein granules

2 cups shredded soy Monterey Jack

1 cup shredded soy cheddar

1 onion, chopped

½ cup soy sour cream

2 tablespoons chopped fresh parsley (optional)

¼ teaspoon pepper

*Enchilada sauce:*

One 15-ounce can tomato sauce

⅔ cup water

⅓ cup chopped green pepper

1 tablespoon chili powder

½ teaspoon oregano

¼ teaspoon ground cumin

1 clove garlic, minced

Twelve 8-inch flour tortillas

¼ cup shredded soy cheddar, for topping

Per Serving: Calories 531, Protein 31 g, Soy Protein 23 g, Fat 21 g, Carbohydrates 55 g, Sodium 1388 mg

Main Dishes

# Mexican-Style Hash

*Yield: 6 servings:*

*This dish goes great with jalapeño cornbread.*

1 cup beef-style textured soy protein granules

2 teaspoons vegetarian beef-flavored broth powder or equivalent

1 cup water

1 onion, finely chopped

2 tablespoons canola oil

2 cups finely chopped potatoes

1½ cups frozen corn kernels, thawed

One 10¾-ounce can condensed tomato soup

½ cup grated soy cheddar

½ teaspoon pepper

1½ teaspoons chili powder

Combine the textured soy protein, broth powder, and water in a saucepan. Bring to a boil and let stand for 10 minutes.

In a large skillet, sauté the onion in the oil until tender. Add the soy granule mixture, potatoes, corn, condensed soup, cheese, pepper, and chili powder, and stir well.

Preheat the oven to 350°F. Place the soy granule mixture into an oiled 1½ quart casserole dish, and bake for 45 to 60 minutes, or until the potatoes are done and the top has browned.

Main Dishes

Per Serving: Calories 201, Protein 13 g, Soy Protein 9 g, Fat 7 g, Carbohydrates 26 g, Sodium 581 mg

# Southwestern Seasoned Loaf

*Yield: 8 servings*

*Slices of this loaf make great sandwiches.*

In a medium saucepan, bring the 2 cups water to a boil. Add the broth powder, seasoning, and textured soy granules. Let stand for 10 minutes.

Mix the egg replacer with the combread stuffing, onion, minced garlic, garlic powder, green chiles, chili powder, cornmeal, ½ cup of the tomato sauce, and the reconstituted granules. Mix thoroughly.

Preheat the oven to 350°F. Place the green pepper slices in the bottom of an oiled loaf pan. Add the textured soy mixture, and press firmly in pan. Mix the remaining tomato sauce, allspice, and Worcestershire sauce, and spread on top of the loaf. Bake for 45 minutes, then remove from the oven and cool for 15 minutes. Run a knife around the edge of the loaf to loosen, then invert onto a serving dish.

2 cups water

4 teaspoons vegetarian beef-flavored broth powder or equivalent

1 teaspoon Cajun seasoning or Harvest Direct Sausage Seasoning, p. 8

2 cups beef-style textured soy protein granules

Egg replacer equivalent to 1 egg

1 cup cornbread stuffing mix

1 onion, chopped

1 clove garlic, minced

¼ teaspoon garlic powder

4 ounces green chiles, minced

1 tablespoon chili powder

½ cup cornmeal

1 cup tomato sauce

½ large green pepper, sliced

Pinch allspice

½ teaspoon anchovy-free Worcestershire sauce

Per Serving: Calories 165, Protein 15 g, Soy Protein 10 g, Fat 3 g, Carbohydrates 26 g, Sodium 500 mg

Main Dishes

# San Antone-Style Fajitas

*Enjoy this speedy version of fajitas; top with tomatoes, lettuce, and sautéed onions.*

2 cups water

3 tablespoons vegetarian beef-flavored broth powder or equivalent

2 teaspoons Dijon mustard

2 tablespoons soy sauce

2 cups beef-style textured soy protein strips

¼ cup canola oil

1 bunch green onions, cut into 1-inch pieces

4 large cloves garlic, thinly sliced

1 tablespoon sesame seeds

12 flour tortillas

¼ cup chopped cilantro

In a medium saucepan, bring the water to a boil. Add the vegetarian beef-flavored broth, Dijon mustard, and soy sauce. Add the textured soy strips, reduce to a simmer, and cook for 10 minutes.

In a large nonstick skillet, heat the oil. Add the green onions, garlic, and sesame seeds. Sauté over medium high heat for 3 minutes. Add the soy strips and continue to sauté for 5 more minutes. Serve in the flour tortillas with the cilantro, and top with salsa.

*Main Dishes*

Per Serving: Calories 355 Protein 19 g, Soy Protein 15 g, Fat 14 g, Carbohydrates 37 g, Sodium 828 mg

# Spicy Corn-Cheese Pie

*Yield: 6 servings*

*Even with all the ingredients, this comes together quickly.*

In a medium saucepan, bring the 1 cup water to a boil. Add the broth powder and textured soy granules; mix well and let stand 10 minutes.

Stir in the corn, green pepper, onion, cornmeal, oregano, chili powder, pepper, tomato sauce, and half the green chiles. Set aside.

To make the crust, combine the flour and 2 tablespoons cornmeal. Cut in the margarine or oil with 2 knives or a pastry blender until the mixture is the size of small peas. Sprinkle 3 to 4 tablespoons cold water over the mixture, and stir with a fork until the dough holds together. Form into a ball and flatten to ½-inch thick; keep the edges smooth. Roll out on a floured surface to a diameter 1½ inches larger than an inverted 9-inch pie plate. Fit the dough into the pie plate, fold the edges to form a rim, then flute the edges.

Preheat the oven to 425°F. Place the textured soy mixture into the pie shell, and bake for 25 minutes. Mix the egg replacer with the milk,

1 cup water

2 teaspoons vegetarian beef-flavored broth powder or equivalent

1 cup beef-style textured soy protein granules

1 cup canned corn

¼ cup finely chopped green bell pepper

¼ cup finely chopped onions

¼ cup cornmeal

½ teaspoon oregano

1 teaspoon chili powder

⅛ teaspoon pepper

One 8-ounce can tomato sauce

¼ cup chopped green chiles

Egg replacer equivalent to 1 egg

¼ cup nondairy milk

½ teaspoon dry mustard

½ teaspoon anchovy-free Worcestershire sauce

Main Dishes

1½ cups shredded nondairy cheddar

¼ cup sliced black olives

2 tablespoons bacon-flavored soy bits

*Piecrust*

1 cup flour

2 tablespoons cornmeal

⅓ cup dairy-free margarine or oil

3 to 4 tablespoons cold water

dry mustard, Worcestershire sauce, shredded cheese, half the sliced olives, and the remaining green chiles. Remove the pie from the oven, and spread the cheese mixture on top. Sprinkle with the Bacon Flavored Bits and remaining olives. Bake for 5 minutes or until the cheese is melted and bubbly. Let stand 10 minutes before slicing.

Per Serving: Calories 370, Protein 20 g, Soy Protein 15 g, Fat 16 g, Carbohydrates 35 g, Sodium 387 mg

# Indian Curry Stew

*Yield: 4 servings*

*An Indian flat bread or pita bread is excellent on the side.*

In a small saucepan, bring the water to a boil. Add the broth powder and mix well. Add the textured soy chunks, and simmer for 15 minutes.

Melt the margarine in a large saucepan, and heat the turmeric, curry powder, coriander, ginger, chili powder and pepper until the spices start to sizzle. Add the onions and sauté over medium heat until limp. Add the remaining ingredients, including the textured soy chunks, and cook over medium heat until the celery is tender but still slightly crisp. The vegetables will give off some juices as they cook. Serve over rice.

2 cups water

3 tablespoons vegetarian chicken-flavored broth powder or equivalent

2 cups unflavored textured soy protein chunks

3 tablespoons dairy-free margarine

1 teaspoon ground turmeric

1 teaspoon curry powder

1 teaspoon coriander

½ teaspoon ground ginger

⅛ teaspoon chili powder

⅛ teaspoon pepper

2 onions, finely chopped

2 tomatoes, chopped

2 green bell peppers, chopped

1 celery stalk, chopped

2 cloves garlic, minced

3 parsley sprigs, minced

⅓ cup seedless raisins

1 tablespoon dry sherry

1½ teaspoons lemon juice

Main Dishes

Per Serving: Calories 268, Protein 27 g, Soy Protein 14 g, Fat 6 g, Carbohydrates 37 g, Sodium 777 mg

# Far East Vegetable & Noodle Sauté

*Yield: 4 servings*

*Lo mein or spaghetti noodles can be used in place of angel hair pasta.*

½ cup water

½ cup beef-style textured soy protein granules

2 teaspoons vegetarian beef-flavored broth powder or equivalent

3 tablespoons dairy-free margarine

¼ cup blanched almonds

¼ cup broccoli, cooked and drained

¼ cup chopped onions

¼ cup snow peas

¼ cup chopped red and green bell peppers

¼ cup sliced mushrooms

I clove garlic, chopped

I½ cups water

¼ cup teriyaki sauce

I teaspoon sweetener

4 ounces angel hair pasta

In a small saucepan, bring the ½ cup water to a boil. Add the textured soy granules and broth powder to the water; remove from the heat, and let stand 10 minutes.

In a large skillet or wok, melt the margarine over medium high heat. Add the almonds and sauté until browned. Remove the almonds and set aside.

Add the vegetables and garlic to the skillet, and sauté 3 minutes. Add the 1½ cups water, teriyaki sauce, sweetener, and pasta. Cover and simmer for 3 minutes or until the pasta is tender. Add the textured soy granules, and simmer until warm.

Per Serving: Calories 260, Protein 13 g, Soy Protein 5 g, Fat 10 g, Carbohydrates 34 g, Sodium 924 mg

# Egg Rolls

*Yield: 20 eggrolls*

In a small saucepan, bring the ½ cup water to a boil. Add the textured soy granules and broth powder, and mix well. Remove from the heat and let stand for 10 minutes.

Soak the dried mushrooms in enough boiling water to cover for 20 minutes. Drain, remove the stems, and shred. Heat 2 tablespoons of the oil in large nonstick skillet or wok, and stir-fry the ginger and green onions for 30 seconds. Add the textured soy granules, 1 tablespoon of the soy sauce, the sugar, sherry, and pepper. Stir-fry 1 minute, remove from the pan, and set aside.

Heat the remaining 3 tablespoons of oil in the skillet or wok. Stir-fry the cabbage, soaked mushrooms, celery, and bean sprouts until tender and crisp. Add the soy granule mixture to the vegetable mixture, along with the remaining 1 tablespoon soy sauce, and stir until thoroughly heated. Remove from the pan and drain in a colander. Let stand until cool.

Preheat the oven to 350°F. Mix the cornstarch with the 2 tablespoons water. Put 2 heaping teaspoons of the filling mixture on

½ cup water

½ cup beef-style textured soy protein granules

1 teaspoon vegetarian beef-flavored broth powder or equivalent

¼ cup dried shiitake or wood ear mushrooms

5 tablespoons canola oil

½ teaspoon ground ginger

2 green onions, chopped

2 tablespoons soy sauce

1 teaspoon sugar

1 tablespoon sherry

½ teaspoon pepper

½ small head cabbage, shredded

¼ cup chopped celery

½ pound bean sprouts

1 tablespoon cornstarch

2 tablespoons water

20 egg roll skins

Per 2 eggrolls: Calories 206, Protein 6 g, Soy Protein 2 g, Fat 10 g, Carbohydrates 24 g, Sodium 226 mg

Main Dishes

each egg roll wrapper. Fold the bottom of the wrapper over the filling, then the two sides. Roll away from you to close the top, and seal the edges of the wrapper with the dissolved corn-starch. Place the egg rolls seam side down on oiled baking sheets, and brush with oil. Bake for 20 minutes, then turn over the egg rolls and bake an additional 20 minutes.

# Hot Orange Soy Chunks

*Yield: 4 servings*

*You can leave out the jalapeño pepper for a milder flavor.*

2 cups water

3 tablespoons vegetarian chicken-flavored broth powder or equivalent

2 tablespoons Dijon mustard

2 tablespoons orange marmalade

1 jalapeño pepper, seeded and minced

2 teaspoons fresh lime juice

1 teaspoon sliced black olives

2 cups unflavored textured soy protein chunks

In a small saucepan, bring the water to a boil. Add the broth powder and mix thoroughly. Combine the mustard, marmalade, jalapeño, lime juice, and olives with the broth mixture, and bring to a boil. Remove from the heat, add the soy chunks, and let stand for 10 minutes.

Preheat the oven to 350° F. Place the mixture in a 1½-quart baking dish, and bake for 35 to 40 minutes, or until the soy chunks are tender. Baste once during cooking with the mustard and marmalade mixture. Serve with rice.

Per Serving: Calories 182, Protein 25 g, Soy Protein 15 g, Fat 2 g, Carbohydrates 26 g, Sodium 487 mg

# Citrus Chunks

Yield: 6 servings

*Add 1 teaspoon of chili sauce for a spicier version of this.*

Drain the pineapple and set the juice aside. In a mixing bowl, make a citrus sauce by combining the pineapple juice, garlic, cornstarch, Worcestershire sauce, mustard, and rosemary; set aside.

In a small saucepan, bring the water to a boil, and add the broth powder and ¼ cup of the pineapple juice mixture; mix well. Add the soy protein chunks, and simmer for 15 minutes.

Preheat the oven to 350°F. Place the cooked soy chunks in a shallow 9 x 13-inch baking dish. Stir in the remaining pineapple juice mixture, and pour over the chunks. Bake for 25 minutes. Mix the pineapple chunks with the soy protein mixture in the baking dish. Place the lemon slices on top, baste with the sauce in the pan, and continue baking 5 minutes longer. Serve with rice.

One 20-ounce can pineapple chunks in juice

2 cloves garlic, minced

1 tablespoon cornstarch

1 teaspoon anchovy-free Worcestershire sauce

2 teaspoons Dijon mustard

1 teaspoon dried rosemary

2 cups water

3 tablespoons vegetarian chicken-flavored broth powder or equivalent

2 cups unflavored textured soy protein chunks

1 lemon, thinly sliced

Main Dishes

Per Serving: Calories 167, Protein 17 g, Soy Protein 10 g, Fat 1 g, Carbohydrates 31 g, Sodium 286 mg

# Down-Home Barbecued Chunks

*Yield: 4 servings*

*Baked potato wedges and corn on the cob make this a complete summer meal.*

1 cup ketchup

½ cup chopped white onions

¼ cup brown sugar

¼ cup maple syrup or brown rice syrup

¼ cup water

2 tablespoons yellow mustard

2 tablespoons anchovy-free Worcestershire sauce

½ teaspoon Cajun seasoning

½ teaspoon minced garlic

½ jalapeño, seeded and finely diced

1 cup beef-style textured soy protein chunks

In a medium saucepan, combine all the ingredients, except the textured soy chunks. Bring the mixture to a boil, then reduce the heat. Add the chunks and let simmer 10 minutes.

Preheat the oven to 350°F. Place the soy chunk mixture into a 9 x 9-inch baking dish, cover, and bake for 20 minutes. Serve as a sandwich filling or eat it solo!

NOTE: For a milder version, reduce the amount of jalapeño.

Per Serving: Calories 243, Protein 13 g, Soy Protein 10 g, Fat 0.8 g, Carbohydrates 53 g, Sodium 998 mg

Main Dishes

# Beef-Style Burgundy Stew

*Yield: 8 servings*

In a mixing bowl, combine the wine, olive oil, pepper, thyme, and bay leaf. Add 1 cup of the wine mixture to the water, and set the remainder of the mixture aside. Bring the water mixture to a boil, and add the 2 teaspoons broth powder and textured soy chunks. Stir well and set aside for 10 to 15 minutes. Drain the excess marinade from the chunks, and add to the wine mixture previously set aside. Place the chunks in a 9 x 13-inch casserole dish.

Preheat the oven to 350°F. Melt 2 tablespoons of the margarine in a skillet, and sauté the onions, carrots, and garlic until lightly browned, about 5 minutes. Blend in the flour and stir 1 minute. Add the remaining marinade, 4 teaspoons broth powder, and tomato paste. Stir the mixture until it comes to a boil, and pour it over the chunks. Cover and bake for 45 minutes.

While the chunks are cooking, parboil the pearl onions and remove their outer skins. Melt the remaining tablespoon of margarine in a skillet. Add the sugar and sauté the pearl onions until golden. Add in the mushrooms and sauté for 2 more minutes. Combine with the tomatoes and add to the textured soy chunks. Continue to bake for 15 minutes.

2 cups red wine

2 tablespoons olive oil

1 teaspoon pepper

½ teaspoon ground thyme

1 bay leaf

1 cup water

2 teaspoons vegetarian beef-flavored broth powder or equivalent

2 cups beef-style textured soy protein chunks

3 tablespoons dairy-free margarine

2 onions, finely chopped

2 carrots, finely chopped

2 cloves garlic, finely chopped

¼ cup flour

4 teaspoons vegetarian beef-flavored broth powder or equivalent

1 tablespoon tomato paste

1½ cups pearl onions

¼ teaspoon sugar

2 ounces mushrooms, sliced

One 14½-ounce can stewed tomatoes, drained and chopped

Per Serving: Calories 218, Protein 9 g, Soy Protein 7 g, Fat 7 g, Carbohydrates 19 g, Sodium 182 mg

Main Dishes

# Irish Stew

Yield: 4 servings

*Breads are always a must with stews. Biscuits are great with this one*

1 cup beef-style textured soy protein chunks

1⅓ cups water

4 teaspoons vegetarian beef-flavored broth powder or equivalent

1 bay leaf

½ teaspoon pepper

1 teaspoon anchovy-free Worcestershire sauce

3 tablespoons dairy-free margarine

⅓ cup chopped onion

1 clove garlic, minced

⅓ cup sliced carrots

1 cup cubed potatoes

⅓ cup sliced celery

¼ cup frozen peas

1 tablespoon flour

¼ cup water

2 tablespoons dried parsley

In a medium saucepan, simmer the textured soy chunks in the 1⅓ cups water, broth powder, bay leaf, pepper, and Worcestershire sauce for 20 minutes.

In another pan, melt the margarine and sauté the vegetables until the onions are limp. Add the vegetables to the soy chunk mixture, cover, and cook until the vegetables are tender, about 10 to 15 minutes. Combine the flour and the ¼ cup cold water. Add to the stew mixture along with the parsley, and stir until the liquid is smooth and thick.

Main Dishes

Per Serving: Calories 142, Protein 14 g, Soy Protein 10 g, Fat 5 g, Carbohydrates 19 g, Sodium 350 mg

# Milwaukee Beef-Style Stew

*Yield: 6 servings*

*Add hot pepper sauce to this for a little kick.*

In a small saucepan, bring the water to a boil. Add the broth powder and mix well. Stir in the textured soy chunks, remove from the heat, and let stand for 10 minutes.

Preheat the oven to 375°F. Melt the margarine in a medium skillet, add the onions, and sauté over medium heat until limp. Add the garlic and sauté 2 minutes longer.

In a 9 x 13-inch baking dish, combine the textured soy chunks, onion, garlic, and remaining ingredients. Bake for 45 minutes or until the top is browned.

1 cup water

4 teaspoons vegetarian beef-flavored broth powder or equivalent

1 cup beef-style textured soy protein chunks

2 tablespoons dairy-free margarine

3 onions, coarsely chopped

2 cloves garlic, minced

1 can beer or nonalcoholic beer

1½ tablespoons red wine vinegar

1 bay leaf

½ teaspoon dried thyme

½ teaspoon pepper

1½ cups frozen corn, thawed

1 tablespoon sweetener

Per Serving: Calories 141, Protein 6 g, Soy Protein 5 g, Fat 5 g, Carbohydrates 20 g, Sodium 149 mg

# Mediterranean Stew

*Serve this with toasted country-style bread to sop up the flavorful sauce.*

1 cup water

4 teaspoons vegetarian beef-flavored broth powder or equivalent

1 cup beef-style textured soy protein chunks

2 potatoes, cubed

3 carrots, peeled and diced

1 turnip, peeled and cubed

1 large clove garlic, minced

1 teaspoon ground cumin

½ teaspoon ground turmeric

½ teaspoon pepper

½ tablespoon tomato paste

3 cups water

In a small saucepan, bring the water to a boil. Add the broth powder and mix well. Stir in the textured soy chunks, remove from the heat, and let stand for 10 minutes.

Preheat the oven to 400°F. Combine the soy chunks and remaining ingredients in a 9 x 13-inch baking dish. Bake for 1 hour or until the vegetables are tender.

Main Dishes

Per Serving: Calories 87, Protein 9 g, Soy Protein 5 g, Fat 0 g, Carbohydrates 17 g, Sodium 167 mg

# Stir-Fried Chunks in Ginger-Tomato Sauce

*Yield: 4 servings*

*Use as a topping for lo mein or spaghetti noodles.*

In a small saucepan, bring the 1 cup water to a boil. Stir in the broth powder, 2 tablespoons of the cornstarch, the 2 tablespoons soy sauce, and sherry. Add the textured soy chunks, and simmer for 15 minutes, or until the sauce is mostly absorbed Add the remaining ½ tablespoon cornstarch to the textured soy protein.

In a medium nonstick skillet, heat the oil over high heat. Slowly add the textured soy chunk mixture, and cook until lightly browned. Drain and remove the chunks from the skillet, and set aside. Make sure to keep the leftover oil in the skillet.

Add the onions and ginger, and sauté for 30 seconds over medium-high heat. Stir in the mushrooms, celery, bamboo shoots, carrots, and ¼ cup water. Stir-fry until the vegetables are cooked and the liquid is reduced. Add the textured soy chunks.

Combine the ketchup, 1 tablespoon soy sauce, 1 tablespoon sugar, 6 tablespoons water, 2 teaspoons cornstarch, and pepper. Add to the chunks and vegetable mixture, and cook over high heat until the sauce is thick. Remove from the heat and serve on rice.

1 cup water

4 teaspoons vegetarian beef-flavored broth powder or equivalent

2½ tablespoons cornstarch

2 tablespoons soy sauce

1 tablespoon sherry

1 cup beef-style textured soy protein chunks

¼ cup canola oil

2 green onions, cut into 2-inch pieces

1 tablespoon minced fresh gingerroot

½ cup chopped mushrooms

½ cup diced celery

½ cup diced bamboo shoots

1 cup diced carrots

¼ cup water

4 tablespoons ketchup

1 tablespoon soy sauce

1 tablespoon sugar

6 tablespoons water

2 teaspoons cornstarch

¼ teaspoon pepper

Per Serving: Calories 254, Protein 9 g, Soy Protein 9 g, Fat 13 g, Carbohydrates 23 g, Sodium 1097 mg

*Main Dishes*

# Spicy Water Chestnuts with Soy Chunks

*Yield: 4 servings*

*A cup of chopped cabbage is a simple and nice addition to this.*

1 cup water

4 teaspoons vegetarian beef-flavored broth powder or equivalent

1 tablespoon sherry

2 tablespoons soy sauce

2½ tablespoons cornstarch

¼ cup water

1 cup beef-style textured soy protein chunks

¼ cup canola oil

2 tablespoons chopped green onion

1½ tablespoons minced ginger

1½ tablespoons minced garlic

1 teaspoon minced red chiles

4 ounces canned water chestnuts, drained and chopped

1 tablespoon sherry

2 tablespoons soy sauce

3 tablespoons water

4 teaspoons sugar

2 teaspoons cornstarch

2 teaspoons white vinegar

1 teaspoon sesame seeds

½ teaspoon pepper

In a small saucepan, bring the 1 cup water to a boil. Stir in the broth powder, 1 tablespoon sherry, and 2 tablespoons soy sauce.

Mix 2 tablespoons of the cornstarch with the ¼ cup water, and add to the broth mixture. Add the textured soy chunks, and simmer for 15 minutes, or until the sauce has thickened. Add the remaining ½ tablespoon cornstarch to the soy chunks.

Heat the oil in a medium nonstick skillet over high heat. Stir-fry the textured soy chunks until lightly browned. Drain the oil from the chunks, set them aside, and return the oil to the skillet. To the remaining oil, add the green onion, ginger, garlic, and chiles. Stir-fry for 30 seconds, then add the water chestnuts and soy chunks. Combine the remaining ingredients and add to the soy chunks and water chestnuts. Heat until the sauce has thickened, and serve over rice.

*Main Dishes*

Per Serving: Calories 246, Protein 9 g, Soy Protein 9 g, Fat 13 g, Carbohydrates 19 g, Sodium 1152 mg

# Pepper Strips

Yield: 4 servings

*This is a great summer recipe, when green peppers are abundant in the garden.*

Combine all the ingredients, except the textured soy strips and green peppers, in large saucepan. Bring to a boil over medium heat, and add the soy strips. Remove from the heat and let stand for 10 minutes.

Add the green peppers, cover, and simmer over low heat for 45 minutes, or until the strips are tender and the sauce has thickened.

1 small onion, minced

2 cloves garlic, minced

3 tablespoons vegetarian beef-flavored broth powder or equivalent

2 cups water

4 tablespoons soy sauce

1 teaspoon ground ginger

2 teaspoons anchovy-free Worcestershire sauce

½ teaspoon pepper

1 cup beef-style textured soy protein strips

2 green peppers, sliced into ¼-inch strips

Main Dishes

Per Serving: Calories 83, Protein 10 g, Soy Protein 10 g, Fat 0 g, Carbohydrates 9 g, Sodium 1336 mg

# Hungarian-style Goulash

*This recipe was adapted from a four-generation family favorite.*

1 cup water

4 teaspoons vegetarian beef flavored broth powder or equivalent

1 cup beef-style textured soy protein strips

2 medium onions, chopped

3 tablespoons oil

1/2 cup ketchup

3 tablespoons anchovy-free Worchestershire sauce

2 tablespoons brown sugar

1 teaspoon paprika

1/4 teaspoon cayenne pepper

1/2 cup water

1/4 teaspoon pepper

1 teaspoon vinegar

1/4 cup water

2 tablespoons flour

In a small saucepan, bring the 1 cup water to a boil. Add the broth powder and textured soy strips, mix thoroughly, and set aside for 10 minutes.

In a medium saucepan, sauté the onions in the oil until limp and transparent. Add all the ingredients except for the 1/4 cup water and the flour. Simmer for 30 minutes over medium heat.

Mix the 1/4 cup cold water and flour until well blended. Add to the textured soy mixture and mix thoroughly. Cook over medium heat until thick and bubbly. Serve over noodles.

Main Dishes

Per Serving: Calories 253, Protein 14 g, Soy Protein 8 g, Fat 11 g, Carbohydrates 34 g, Sodium 691 mg

# West African Beef-Style Curry

*Yield: 6 servings*

*The exotic, aromatic smell of spices will entice any appetite.*

In a small saucepan, bring the 1 cup water to a boil. Add the 4 teaspoons broth powder and textured soy strips, and let stand for 10 minutes.

Mix the flour with the paprika, cayenne pepper, and chili powder. Add the textured soy strips to the flour mixture, and toss. Make sure the strips are well-coated.

In a large saucepan, heat the 3 tablespoons oil and sauté the onions until limp. Add the coconut, curry powder, garlic, Tabasco, 3 cups water, and 6 teaspoons broth powder. Cook over medium heat.

In a medium nonstick skillet, heat the ¼ cup oil, and sauté the textured soy strips for 3 minutes. Add this to the curry mixture, and simmer for 30 minutes, stirring occasionally. Serve over rice.

1 cup water

4 teaspoons vegetarian beef-flavored broth powder or equivalent

1 cup beef-style textured soy protein strips

½ cup flour

¼ teaspoon paprika

¼ teaspoon cayenne pepper

¼ teaspoon chili powder

3 tablespoons canola oil

2 onions, chopped

2½ tablespoons coconut

4 tablespoons curry powder

1 clove garlic, minced

4 drops Tabasco sauce

3 cups water

6 teaspoons vegetarian beef-flavored broth powder or equivalent

¼ cup canola oil

Main Dishes

Per Serving: Calories 249, Protein 11 g, Soy Protein 6 g, Fat 18 g, Carbohydrates 22 g, Sodium 527 mg

# Szechwan-Style Strips

*Yield: 4 servings*

*The spicy Szechwan dishes at Chinese restaurants served as inspiration for this recipe.*

1 cup water

4 teaspoons vegetarian beef-flavored broth powder or equivalent

2½ teaspoons soy sauce

1 tablespoon cornstarch

1½ teaspoons canola oil

1 cup beef-style textured soy protein strips

¼ cup canola oil

4 carrots, julienned

2 cloves garlic, minced

3 red chiles, minced

4 green onions, cut into 2-inch strips

2½ teaspoons sherry

1½ teaspoons white vinegar

2½ teaspoons sugar

3 teaspoons soy sauce

In a small saucepan, bring the water to a boil, then add the broth powder. Combine the 2½ teaspoons soy sauce, 1 tablespoon cornstarch, and 1½ teaspoons oil, and add to the boiling water. Add the textured soy strips, and simmer for 15 minutes or until the sauce has thickened.

Heat the ¼ cup oil in a medium nonstick pan over medium-high heat. Stir-fry the carrots for 5 minutes or until crisp. Remove the carrots from the oil. In the remaining oil, stir-fry the textured soy strips until lightly browned. Remove and add to the carrots. In the remaining oil, add the garlic and stir-fry for 30 seconds. Add the chiles and green onions, and stir for 30 more seconds. Mix in the soy strips and carrots. Combine the sherry, vinegar, sugar, and 3 teaspoons soy sauce. Add to the textured soy strips and carrots, and stir-fry for 30 seconds. Remove from the pan and serve on rice.

Main Dishes

Per Serving: Calories 242, Protein 9 g, Soy Protein 8 g, Fat 15 g, Carbohydrates 17 g, Sodium 674 mg

# Oriental Stir-Fry with Black Bean Sauce

*Yield: 4 servings*

*The bean sauce gives this Oriental recipe its robust flavor.*

Have all the vegetables prepared before you start this recipe.

In a small saucepan, bring the 1 cup water to a boil. Add the broth powder and textured soy strips, combine well, and let stand 10 minutes.

Combine the sherry, black bean sauce, ¼ cup water, sugar, cayenne pepper, and cornstarch in a small bowl. Mix well and set aside. In a medium nonstick skillet or wok, heat the oil over medium heat. Stir in the ginger and garlic, and sauté for 1 minute. Add the soy strips and broccoli, and continue cooking for 3 minutes. Add the peppers, green onions, and celery, and cook for 3 minutes. Then add the cornstarch mixture, cook for 3 minutes, and add the water chestnuts and cook for 1 more minute.

1 cup water

2 teaspoons vegetarian beef-flavored broth powder or equivalent

1 cup beef-style textured soy protein strips

3 tablespoons dry sherry

¼ cup black bean sauce

¼ cup water

½ tablespoon sugar

¼ teaspoon cayenne pepper

1 tablespoon cornstarch

3 tablespoons canola oil

½ teaspoon ground ginger

1 clove garlic, minced

1 pound broccoli stalks, sliced

½ red bell pepper, julienned

½ green bell pepper, julienned

6 green onions, diagonally cut

2 celery stalks, cut in 1-inch pieces

¼ cup chopped canned water chestnuts

Per Serving: Calories 301, Protein 19 g, Soy Protein 7 g, Fat 12 g, Carbohydrates 37 g, Sodium 364 mg

Main Dishes

# Waste-No-Time Chiken Breasts

*Yield: 4 servings*

*This recipe also makes an excellent sandwich.*

4 textured soy Chiken Breasts

I to 2 tablespoons vegetarian chicken-flavored broth powder or equivalent

3 cups water

½ teaspoon salt

I teaspoon ground pepper

½ teaspoon chili powder

½ teaspoon cayenne pepper

½ teaspoon dried thyme

½ teaspoon dried basil

½ teaspoon dried garlic

½ teaspoon anchovy-free Worcestershire sauce (optional)

Combine the Chiken Breasts, broth powder, and water in a medium saucepan. Bring to a boil, cover, and simmer for 35 to 40 minutes or until tender.

In a medium skillet, bring 2 tablespoons of the broth from cooking the Chiken Breasts to a simmer over medium heat. Add the remaining ingredients (except the Chiken Breasts) to the skillet, and combine. Remove the Breasts from the broth, and heat in the skillet for 5 to 7 minutes, turning once, then remove from the heat and serve.

Main Dishes

Per Serving: Calories 60, Protein 11 g, Soy Protein 10 g, Fat 0 g, Carbohydrates 4 g, Sodium 431 mg

# Ultimate Chiken Breast Sandwiches

Yield: 4 servings

*Topping these with a slice of melted soy cheese makes the super-ultimate sandwich!*

Combine the Chiken Breasts, broth powder, and water in a medium saucepan. Bring to a boil, cover, and simmer for 35 to 40 minutes or until tender.

While the Chiken Breasts are simmering, make a marinade by combining the Cajun seasoning, Worcestershire sauce, soy sauce, sweetener, Dijon mustard, and white wine in a shallow dish. Remove the Chiken Breasts from the broth, place in the marinade, and let stand for 30 minutes to 2 hours in the refrigerator.

Remove the Chiken Brests from the marinade, and heat in a lightly oiled skillet or grill until warm. Arrange on the bottoms of the buns, and top with the tomato slices, lettuce, and sprouts. Spread the remaining marinade on the bun tops, and serve.

4 textured soy Chiken Breasts

1 to 2 tablespoons vegetarian chicken-flavored broth powder or equivalent

3 cups water

1 teaspoon Cajun seasoning

1 tablespoon anchovy-free Worcestershire sauce

1 tablespoon soy sauce

1 tablespoon sweetener

2 tablespoons Dijon mustard

2 tablespoons white wine

4 tomato slices

4 romaine lettuce leaves

½ cup your favorite sprouts

4 whole wheat buns, sliced in half

Main Dishes

Per Serving: Calories 215, Protein 15 g, Soy Protein 10 g, Fat 2 g, Carbohydrates 31 g, Sodium 872 mg

# Chiken Breasts with Chicken-Style Gravy

*Yield: 4 servings*

*For a homestyle meal, serve with mashed potatoes on the side.*

4 textured soy Chiken Breasts

4 tablespoons vegetarian chicken-flavored broth powder or equivalent

3 cups water

2 tablespoons flour

2 tablespoons dairy-free margarine

1½ cups water

Combine the Chiken Breasts, 2 tablespoons of the broth powder, and 3 cups water in a medium saucepan. Bring to a boil, cover, and simmer for 35 to 40 minutes or until tender.

While the Breasts are simmering, melt the margarine in a medium skillet over medium heat. Add the remaining 2 tablespoons broth powder and the flour to the skillet, and stir until smooth. Slowly add the 1½ cups water while stirring. Bring the gravy to a simmer, and cook for 2 to 3 minutes or until it begins to thicken. Remove the Chiken Breasts from the broth, cover with the gravy, and serve.

Per Serving: Calories 138, Protein 12 g, Soy Protein 10 g, Fat 5 g, Carbohydrates 7 g, Sodium 506 mg

Main Dishes

# Sunshine State Grilled Chiken Breasts

*Yield: 4 servings*

*These are delicious on top of mixed greens with a citrus salad dressing.*

Combine the Chiken Breasts, broth powder, and water in a medium saucepan. Bring to a boil, cover, and simmer for 35 to 40 minutes or until tender.

While the Chiken Breasts are simmering, make a marinade by combining the remaining ingredients in a shallow bowl. Remove the Chiken Breasts from the broth, and place in the marinade. Let stand for 30 minutes to 2 hours.

Grill the Chiken Breasts over medium heat for 3 to 5 minutes per side, basting generously with the remaining marinade. Serve with rice and garnish with fruit slices.

4 textured soy Chiken Breasts

1 to 2 tablespoons vegetarian chicken-flavored broth powder or equivalent

3 cups water

2 tablespoons canola oil

1½ tablespoons honey

2 tablespoons orange juice

2 tablespoons lemon juice

1 tablespoon lime juice

1 teaspoon finely chopped fresh mint

1 teaspoon grated orange zest

½ teaspoon grated lemon zest

½ teaspoon grated lime zest

½ teaspoon ground pepper

½ teaspoon salt

½ teaspoon hot pepper sauce

Main Dishes

Per Serving: Calories 151, Protein 11 g, Soy Protein 10 g, Fat 7 g, Carbohydrates 11 g, Sodium 432 mg

# St. Louis-Style Fried Chiken Breasts

*Yield: 4 servings*

*Serve these on buns with mustard and lettuce for a great sandwich.*

4 textured soy Chiken Breasts

I to 2 tablespoons vegetarian chicken-flavored broth powder or equivalent

3 cups water

⅔ cup flour

½ cup beer or nonalcoholic beer

I teaspoon Cajun seasoning

½ teaspoon salt

½ teaspoon ground pepper

¼ cup canola oil

Egg replacer equivalent to 2 eggs

Combine the Chiken Breasts, broth powder, and water in a medium saucepan. Bring to a boil, cover, and simmer for 35 to 40 minutes or until tender.

While the Chiken Breasts are simmering, make a batter by combining the remaining ingredients, except the canola oil and egg substitute. Mix until smooth.

Remove the Chiken Breasts from the broth, and either drain in a colander or pat dry. Dip in the egg replacer, then dip in the batter, and let the excess batter drizzle back into the bowl.

In a medium nonstick skillet, sauté the Breasts in the canola oil over medium-high heat until golden brown (up to 10 minutes), turning once carefully. Try to avoid cracking the batter when you turn the pieces so the Chiken Breasts will not soak up too much oil.

Main Dishes

Per Serving: Calories 218, Protein 16 g, Soy Protein 10 g, Fat 7 g, Carbohydrates 19 g, Sodium 471 mg

# Louisiana Chiken Breasts Pie

*Yield: 4 servings*

*Louisiana natives wouldn't think of having this without a bottle of Tabasco at the table.*

Combine the Chiken Breasts, broth powder, and 3 cups water in a medium saucepan. Bring to a boil, cover, and simmer for 35 to 40 minutes or until tender.

While the Breasts are simmering, combine 1¼ cups of the flour, the yeast, and salt in a large bowl. Add the 1 cup warm water and 2 tablespoons of the canola oil. Beat with an electric mixer on low for 30 seconds, making sure all the flour is moistened. Continue beating on high for 3 minutes. Stir in as much of the remaining flour as possible. Place on a lightly floured surface, and knead in any remaining flour for about 6 minutes to form a moderately stiff dough that is smooth and elastic. Divide in half, cover, and let rest for 10 minutes.

In a medium saucepan, sauté the potato and onion in the remaining 2 tablespoons canola oil, stirring frequently over medium heat for 5 to 6 minutes or until the onion is tender. Stir in the ⅓ cup flour, the sage, garlic powder, and cayenne pepper, and add the pre-

- 4 textured soy Chiken Breasts
- 1 to 2 tablespoons vegetarian chicken-flavored broth powder or equivalent
- 3 cups water
- 2 cups flour
- 4 tablespoons canola oil
- 1 package active dry yeast
- 1 cup warm water
- ¼ teaspoon salt
- 1 cup chopped potato
- ½ cup chopped white onion
- ⅓ cup flour
- ½ teaspoon dried sage
- ½ teaspoon garlic powder
- ¼ teaspoon cayenne pepper
- 1¼ cups prepared vegetarian beef-flavored broth
- ½ cup frozen peas
- ½ cup frozen carrots

Main Dishes

pared broth slowly while stirring. Add the peas and carrots, and cook for about 5 minutes or until bubbly, stirring frequently. Remove the Chiken Breasts from the broth, and chop into small cubes. Add to the potato mixture.

Preheat the oven to 375°F. On a lightly floured surface, roll each half of the dough into a 13-inch circle, and place on an oiled baking sheet. Place the Chiken Breast mixture on half of each circle to within 1 inch of the edge. Moisten the edges of the dough with water, and fold the dough in half over the filling. Seal the edges by pressing with a fork. Cut slits in the dough to allow the steam to escape, and bake for 30 to 35 minutes, or until the crust is lightly browned.

Main Dishes

Per Serving: Calories 490, Protein 20 g, Soy Protein 10 g, Fat 13 g, Carbohydrates 69 g, Sodium 390 mg

# Cajun-Baked Crispy Chiken Breasts

*Yield: 4 servings*

*One tablespoon of anchovy-free Worcestershire sauce is a nice addition to this.*

Combine the Chiken Breasts, broth powder, and water in a medium saucepan. Bring to a boil, cover, and simmer for 35 to 40 minutes or until tender. While the Chiken Breasts are simmering, combine the remaining ingredients in a plastic bag.

Preheat the oven to 375°F. After the Breasts are hydrated, remove one piece from the broth (leaving the rest in the pan) and place in the bag. Shake to cover completely and place on a greased or non-stick baking sheet. Repeat with remaining pieces. Bake for 5 to 10 minutes on a side, or until crispy.

- 4 textured soy Chiken Breasts
- 2 tablespoons vegetarian chicken-flavored broth powder or equivalent
- 3 cups water
- ½ cup flour
- 1 teaspoon Cajun seasoning
- ½ teaspoon dried thyme
- ½ teaspoon paprika
- ½ teaspoon garlic powder
- ¼ teaspoon black pepper

Main Dishes

Per Serving: Calories 113, Protein 12 g, Soy Protein 10 g, Fat 0 g, Carbohydrates 14 g, Sodium 220 mg

# Pecan-Breaded Breasts Over Mixed Salad Greens

*Yield: 4 servings*

*This is a great dish for brunches.*

4 textured soy Chiken Breasts

1 to 2 tablespoons vegetarian chicken-flavored broth powder or equivalent

3 cups water

½ cup finely ground pecans

½ cup ground wheat flake cereal

1 tablespoon grated lemon zest

1 tablespoon cracked black pepper

¼ teaspoon salt

¼ cup red wine vinegar

¼ cup olive oil

2 tablespoons minced fresh basil

2 tablespoons Dijon mustard

2 tablespoons water

2 tablespoons olive oil

¼ bunch arugula, torn into bite-size pieces

¼ bunch romaine, torn into bite-size pieces

¼ head radicchio, coarsely chopped

Combine the Chiken Breasts, broth powder, and 3 cups water in a medium saucepan. Bring to a boil, cover, and simmer for 35 to 40 minutes or until tender.

Combine the ground pecans, wheat flakes, lemon zest, black pepper, and salt in a shallow bowl. In a blender, make a dressing by processing the red wine vinegar, ¼ cup olive oil, basil, Dijon mustard, and 2 tablespoons water until combined; set aside.

Remove the Chiken Breasts from the broth, slice into 1/4-inch strips, and dredge in the pecan mixture. In a medium nonstick skillet, brown the strips in the 2 tablespoons olive oil over medium heat for about 3 to 5 minutes. Remove from the heat.

Toss the greens in a salad bowl with the dressing. Place the Chiken Breast strips on top, and serve.

Main Dishes

Per Serving: Calories 406, Protein 16 g, Soy Protein 10 g, Fat 30 g, Carbohydrates 14 g, Sodium 511 mg

# Chiken Breasts Dijon

*Yield: 4 servings*

*These make excellent sandwiches; serve on buns with lettuce.*

Combine the Chiken Breasts, broth powder, and water in a medium saucepan. Bring to a boil, cover, and simmer for 35 to 40 minutes or until tender.

While the Breasts are simmering, combine the lemon zest and ground pepper. Remove the Breasts from the broth, and coat both sides with the pepper mixture.

Melt the margarine in a medium nonstick skillet over medium heat, and add 3 tablespoons of the leftover broth mixture. Add the Chiken Breasts to the skillet, and cook for 3 minutes on each side. Place the Breasts on a plate, and set aside. Pour the remaining margarine and broth into a 1-cup measure, and add enough soymilk to equal ⅔ cup. Pour back into the skillet. Combine the flour with the ¼ cup soymilk, and add to the broth and milk mixture in the skillet. Add the mustard to the skillet mixture, and stir thoroughly. Place the Chiken Breasts back in the skillet, and continue stirring and heating until the sauce is thick and bubbly.

4 textured soy Chiken Breasts

1 tablespoon vegetarian chicken-flavored broth powder or equivalent

3 cups water

1 teaspoon grated lemon zest

1 teaspoon ground pepper

2 tablespoons dairy-free margarine

⅔ cup plain soymilk

2 tablespoons flour

¼ cup plain soymilk

1½ tablespoons Dijon mustard

Main Dishes

Per Serving: Calories 148, Protein 12 g, Soy Protein 12 g, Fat 7 g, Carbohydrates 7 g, Sodium 341 mg

# Marsala Chiken Breasts

Yield: 4 servings

*Serve these over white rice or baked potatoes.*

4 textured soy Chiken Breasts

1 to 2 tablespoons vegetarian chicken-flavored broth powder or equivalent

3 cups water

½ cup flour

½ teaspoon ground pepper

3 tablespoons dairy-free margarine

¼ cup minced shallots or green onions

½ cup sliced mushrooms

¼ cup dry marsala or nonalcoholic red wine

¼ cup prepared vegetarian beef-flavored broth

1 teaspoon lemon juice

Combine the Chiken Breasts, broth powder, and water in a medium saucepan. Bring to a a boil, cover, and simmer for 35 to 40 minutes or until tender.

While the Breasts are simmering, combine the flour and pepper in a shallow dish. Remove the Chiken Breasts from the broth, and dredge in the flour mixture.

Melt the margarine in a medium nonstick skillet over medium heat. Add the Chiken Breasts and sauté about 3 minutes on each side until gold brown. Remove from the heat and set aside.

Add the shallots or green onions to the skillet, and sauté until tender. Add the mushrooms and sauté for 3 minutes more. Add the marsala, prepared broth, and lemon juice, and bring to a boil. Reduce the heat and simmer until the sauce reduces slightly, about 3 to 5 minutes. Add the Chiken Breasts back to the skillet, heat for 1 to 2 minutes, and serve.

Main Dishes

Per Serving: Calories 190, Protein 12 g, Soy Protein 10 g, Fat 7 g, Carbohydrates 15 g, Sodium 265 mg

# Chicken Breasts with Mushrooms & Artichokes

Yield: 4 servings

*Garlic mashed potatoes are a great complimentary dish for these.*

Combine the Chiken Breasts, broth powder, and water in a medium saucepan. Bring to a boil, cover, and simmer for 35 to 40 minutes or until tender.

While the Breasts are simmering, sauté the garlic in the olive oil for 2 minutes in a medium skillet over medium heat. Add the mushrooms and artichokes, and simmer for 3 minutes. Add the vermouth or marsala and lemon juice, and simmer for 5 minutes. Add the Chiken Breasts to the skillet, simmer for 3 minutes, and serve.

4 textured soy Chiken Breasts

1 to 2 tablespoons vegetarian chicken-flavored broth powder or equivalent

3 cups water

2 tablespoons olive oil

3 cloves garlic, minced

½ cup sliced mushrooms

One 14-ounce can artichoke hearts, drained and quartered

¼ cup dry vermouth, marsala, or nonalcoholic red wine

2 teaspoons lemon juice

Main Dishes

Per Serving: Calories 168, Protein 12 g, Soy Protein 10 g, Fat 7 g, Carbohydrates 12 g, Sodium 213 mg

# Grilled Chiken Breasts with Tropical Salsa

*Yield: 4 servings*

*Cut these into strips for a tortilla filling.*

4 textured soy Chiken Breasts

1 tablespoon vegetarian chicken-flavored broth powder or equivalent

3 cups water

1 small can pineapple chunks in juice

1 small red onion, peeled and quartered

1 small red bell pepper, quartered and seeded

½ small jalapeño, seeded

¼ cup chopped cilantro

½ teaspoon ground pepper

½ teaspoon salt

2 tablespoons canola oil

Combine the Chiken Breasts, broth powder, and water in a medium saucepan. Bring to a boil, cover, and simmer for 35 to 40 minutes or until tender.

While the Chiken Breasts are simmering, make a fresh salsa by processing the remaining ingredients in a blender until well combined. Pour into a shallow dish.

Remove the Breasts from the broth, place in the salsa, and let stand for 30 minutes to 2 hours. Grill the Chiken Breasts over medium heat for 3 to 5 minutes on a side, basting with the salsa generously. Serve with the remaining salsa.

Main Dishes

Per Serving: Calories 187, Protein 11 g, Soy Protein 10 g, Fat 7 g, Carbohydrates 19 g, Sodium 443 mg

# Jamaican Grilled Chiken Breasts

Yield: 4 servings

*Rice helps mellow the flavor of this spicy entrée.*

Combine the Chiken Breasts, broth powder, and water in a medium saucepan. Bring to a boil, cover, and simmer for 35 to 40 minutes or until tender.

While the Chiken Breasts are simmering, make a marinade by combining the remaining ingredients in a shallow dish. Remove the Breasts from the broth, and place in the marinade. Marinate for 30 minutes to 2 hours, turning once.

Grill the Chiken Breasts over medium heat for 3 to 5 minutes on each side, basting with the marinade generously. Remove from the heat and serve.

4 textured soy Chiken Breasts

1 tablespoon vegetarian chicken-flavored broth powder or equivalent

3 cups water

2 tablespoons olive oil

2 tablespoons vinegar

2 tablespoons orange juice

1 tablespoon lime juice

1 tablespoon sweetener

2 tablespoons finely chopped green onion

1 clove garlic, minced

½ jalapeño, seeded and minced

1 teaspoon dried thyme

1 teaspoon dried sage

½ teaspoon cinnamon

½ teaspoon salt

Per Serving: Calories 136, Protein 10 g, Soy Protein 10 g, Fat 7 g, Carbohydrates 8 g, Sodium 408 mg

Main Dishes

# Lemon Chiken

*Yield: 4 servings*

*Cut into strips and serve with mixed greens for a salad.*

4 textured soy Chiken Breasts

I tablespoon vegetarian chicken-flavored broth powder or equivalent

3 cups water

2 teaspoons soy sauce

3 tablespoons lemon juice

I tablespoon sweetener

¼ teaspoon salt

¼ teaspoon ground pepper

I small onion, chopped

I small red bell pepper, chopped

I teaspoon grated lemon rind

Combine the Chiken Breasts, broth powder, and water in a medium saucepan. Bring to a boil, cover, and simmer for 35 to 40 minutes or until tender. While the Breasts are simmering, combine the soy sauce, lemon juice, sweetener, salt, and pepper, and set aside.

Preheat the oven to 375°F. After the Chiken Breasts have cooked, remove them from the broth, place in a SIZE baking dish, and cover with the lemon juice mixture. Top with the onion, bell pepper, and lemon rind, and bake in the oven for 30 minutes, basting with the lemon juice mixture frequently. Remove from the oven and serve with rice.

Main Dishes

Per Serving: Calories 85, Protein 11 g, Soy Protein 10 g, Fat 0 g, Carbohydrates 10 g, Sodium 412 mg

# Chiken Breasts Cacciatore

*Yield: 4 servings*

*For a family feast, serve these over fettuccine.*

Combine the Chiken Breasts, broth powder, and water in a medium saucepan. Bring to a boil, cover, and simmer for 35 to 40 minutes or until tender. Remove the Breasts from the broth, and dredge in the flour to coat.

In a medium skillet, brown the Breasts for 3 minutes on each side in the olive oil over medium heat. Remove from the skillet and set aside. Add the garlic to the skillet, and sauté for 1 minute. Add the onion, bell pepper, and mushrooms, and sauté until the onions and peppers are tender (about 3 to 5 minutes). Add the remaining ingredients, except the Breasts, to the skillet, and stir until combined.

Preheat the oven to 375°F. Place the Chiken Breasts in a 9 x 9-inch baking dish, and top with the tomato sauce and vegetable mixture. Cover and bake for 20 minutes.

4 textured soy Chiken Breasts

1 to 2 tablespoons vegetarian chicken-flavored broth powder or equivalent

3 cups water

½ cup flour

2 tablespoons olive oil

2 cloves garlic, minced

1 small onion, sliced

1 small green bell pepper, sliced

½ cup sliced mushrooms

One 8-ounce can tomato sauce

½ cup red wine or nonalcoholic red wine

½ teaspoon dried oregano

½ teaspoon dried basil

½ teaspoon ground pepper

Main Dishes

Per Serving: Calories 223, Protein 13 g, Soy Protein 10 g, Fat 7 g, Carbohydrates 21 g, Sodium 538 mg

# Piccata-Style Chiken Breasts

*Yield: 4 servings*

*Be sure and top these with any extra sauce.*

4 textured soy Chiken Breasts

1 to 2 tablespoons vegetarian chicken-flavored broth powder or equivalent

3 cups water

½ cup flour

½ teaspoon ground pepper

½ teaspoon grated lemon rind

½ teaspoon salt

3 tablespoons olive or canola oil

1 clove garlic, chopped

¼ cup dry white wine or nonalcoholic white wine

¼ cup prepared vegetarian chicken-flavored broth

2 tablespoons lemon juice

2 tablespoons chopped fresh parsley

Lemon slices, for garnish

Combine the Chiken Breasts, broth powder, and water in a medium saucepan. Bring to a boil, cover, and simmer for 35 to 40 minutes or until tender.

Combine the flour, pepper, lemon rind, and salt in flat dish. Remove the Chiken Breasts from the broth, and dredge in the flour mixture.

In a medium nonstick skillet, sauté the garlic in the oil over medium heat until golden. Add the floured Breasts to the skillet, and cook until golden brown on each side. Remove the Breasts from the skillet, and set aside.

Add the wine, broth, and lemon juice to the skillet, and bring to a simmer, scraping the browned flour mixture off the bottom of the skillet. Return the Breasts to the skillet, and continue to cook until the sauce thickens, about 2 to 3 minutes. Remove the Breasts from the sauce, and garnish with the parsley and lemon slices, if desired.

Main Dishes

Per Serving: Calories 222, Protein 13 g, Soy Protein 10 g, Fat 9 g, Carbohydrates 17 g, Sodium 444 mg

# Chiken Fajitas

Yield: 4 servings

*Keep a jar of salsa on hand for garnishing these.*

Combine the Chiken Breasts, broth powder, and water in a medium saucepan. Bring to a boil, cover, and simmer for 35 to 40 minutes or until tender.

While the Breasts are simmering, make a marinade by combining the canola oil, lime juice, chili powder, garlic, and onion in a shallow dish. Remove the Breasts from the broth, and add to the marinade. Let stand for at least 30 minutes or up to 2 hours.

After the Chiken Breasts have marinated, grill the Breasts for 3 to 5 minutes on each side over medium-high heat, basting generously with the marinade. Remove from the grill and slice into ¼-inch strips. Heat the tortillas briefly one at a time on the grill, fill with the strips, and serve with the garnishes.

4 textured soy Chiken Breasts

1 to 2 tablespoons vegetarian chicken-flavored broth powder or equivalent

3 cups water

2 tablespoons canola oil

2 tablespoons lime juice

1 teaspoon chili powder

1 clove garlic, minced

1 large onion, sliced

8 flour tortillas

Shredded lettuce, cilantro, and salsa, for garnish

Main Dishes

Per Serving: Calories 396, Protein 19 g, Soy Protein 10 g, Fat 15 g, Carbohydrates 47 g, Sodium 574 mg

# Southwestern Baked Chiken Breasts

*Yield: 4 servings*

*Cut into strips for an excellent tortilla filling.*

4 textured soy Chiken Breasts

1 to 2 tablespoons vegetarian chicken-flavored broth powder or equivalent

3 cups water

One 14-ounce can diced tomatoes, undrained

One 8-ounce can whole kernel corn, drained

One 8-ounce can red kidney beans, drained

½ cup long grain rice

One 4-ounce can diced green chili peppers, drained

½ teaspoon garlic powder

2 tablespoons finely chopped cilantro

Combine the Chiken Breasts, broth powder, and water in a medium saucepan. Bring to a boil, cover, and simmer for 35 to 40 minutes or until tender.

While the Chiken Breasts are simmering, combine the remaining ingredients, except the cilantro, in a large nonstick skillet. Bring to a boil and simmer for 2 minutes, then transfer this vegetable and rice mixture to a 12 x 7-inch baking dish.

Preheat the oven to 350°F. Remove the Chiken Breasts from the broth, and place on top of the vegetable and rice mixture in the baking dish. Top with the cilantro, cover, and bake for 25 minutes. Uncover and bake for 5 to 10 minutes more, or until the rice is tender.

Main Dishes

Per Serving: Calories 263, Protein 18 g, Soy Protein 10 g, Fat 0 g, Carbohydrates 45 g, Sodium 181 mg

# Stuffed Tortillas, Verde Style

*Yield: 4 servings*

*Shredded soy cheese is a great extra in this recipe.*

Combine the Chiken Breasts, broth powder, and water in a medium saucepan. Bring to a boil, cover, and simmer for 35 to 40 minutes or until tender.

While the Chiken Breasts are simmering, combine the rice, the 1 cup prepared broth, garlic, walnuts, and ½ of the cilantro in a medium saucepan. Bring to a boil, cover, and simmer for 20 minutes, or follow the package instructions for the rice.

Preheat the oven to 375°F. Remove the Chiken Breasts from the broth, and slice into ¼-inch strips. Pour 1 can of the chile sauce onto the bottom of a 9 x 13-inch baking dish. Pour the second can of sauce onto a large plate, and dip a tortilla in the sauce. Fill the tortilla with about 2 tablespoons Chiken Breast strips and 2 tablespoons of the rice mixture, roll up, and place seam side down in the baking pan. Proceed the same way with the remaining tortillas and filling. Cover the filled tortillas with the remaining can of chile sauce and cilantro, and bake for 15 minutes.

4 textured soy Chiken Breasts

2 tablespoons vegetarian chicken-flavored broth powder or equivalent

3 cups water

½ cup long grain white rice

1 cup prepared vegetarian chicken-flavored broth

2 cloves garlic, minced

¼ cup finely chopped walnuts

1 bunch cilantro, chopped

12 flour tortillas

Three 4-ounce cans green chile sauce

Per Serving: Calories 463, Protein 21 g, Soy Protein 10 g, Fat 9 g, Carbohydrates 72 g, Sodium 1307 mg

Main Dishes

# Curried Chiken Breast

*Yield: 4 servings*

*As with any curry dish, rice is the perfect compliment.*

4 textured soy Chiken Breasts

I to 2 tablespoons vegetarian chicken-flavored broth powder or equivalent

3 cups water

2 tablespoons canola oil

I red bell pepper, sliced

I small white onion, sliced

2 tablespoons soy sauce

2 tablespoons Japanese rice vinegar

2 teaspoons curry powder

I teaspoon hot pepper sauce

I cup cooked chopped potatoes

I cup coconut milk

I cup prepared vegetarian chicken-flavored broth

2 tablespoons lime juice

½ cup plain soymilk

Combine the Chiken Breasts, broth powder, and water in a medium saucepan. Bring to a boil, cover, and simmer for 35 to 40 minutes or until tender.

While the Breasts are simmering, sauté the bell pepper and onion in the oil in a medium skillet for 3 minutes over medium heat. Add the remaining ingredients, except the soymilk, and bring to a simmer. Remove the Chiken Breasts from the broth, and add to the skillet. Cover and simmer for 10 minutes. Stir in the soymilk, simmer for 5 minutes, and serve.

Main Dishes

Per Serving: Calories 327, Protein 14 g, Soy Protein 19 g, Fat 19 g, Carbohydrates 19 g, Sodium 755 mg

# Ginger Chiken in Lettuce Wraps

*Yield: 4 servings*

*Chopped peanuts are the perfect garnish for these.*

Combine the Chiken Breasts, broth powder, and water in a medium saucepan. Bring to a boil, cover, and simmer for 35 to 40 minutes or until tender.

While the Chiken Breasts are simmering, make a dressing by combining the olive oil, wine vinegar, sweetener, ginger, and pepper; mix well and set aside.

Remove the Chiken Breasts from the broth, and cut into ¼-inch strips. Combine the Breasts, sesame seeds, and sprouts in a medium bowl, and toss with the dressing. Spoon the Chiken mixture onto the lettuce leaves, wrap like tortillas, and serve.

4 textured soy Chiken Breasts

1 tablespoon vegetarian chicken-flavored broth powder or equivalent

3 cups water

¼ cup olive oil

3 tablespoons white wine vinegar

1 tablespoon sweetener

1 teaspoon grated gingerroot

¼ teaspoon ground pepper

2 teaspoons sesame seeds

½ cup your favorite sprouts

8 large lettuce leaves

Main Dishes

Per Serving: Calories 204, Protein 11 g, Soy Protein 10 g, Fat 13 g, Carbohydrates 8 g, Sodium 112 mg

# Grilled Teriyaki Chiken Breasts

*Yield: 4 servings*

*Add pineapple slices for a fruity infusion.*

4 textured soy Chiken Breasts

I tablespoon vegetarian chicken-flavored broth powder or equivalent

3 cups water

½ cup soy sauce

⅓ cup dry sherry

3 tablespoons sweetener

I clove garlic, crushed

½ teaspoon powdered ginger

2 tablespoons canola oil (optional)

Combine the Chiken Breasts, broth powder, and water in a medium saucepan. Bring to a boil, cover, and simmer for 35 to 40 minutes or until tender.

While the Chiken Breasts are cooking, combine the remaining ingredients in a flat dish. When the Breasts have finished simmering, remove them from the broth and place in the soy sauce mixture. Marinate for 30 minutes to 2 hours, turning once.

Grill the Chiken Breasts for 4 minutes on a side over medium heat, basting with the marinade generously. Remove from the grill, cover with the remaining marinade, and serve.

Main Dishes

Per Serving: Calories 142, Protein 14 g, Soy Protein 13 g, Fat 0 g, Carbohydrates 16 g, Sodium 2121 mg

# Quick-n-Zesty Chiken Tenders

*Yield: 3 servings*

*These also make great sandwiches.*

Combine the Chiken Tenders, broth powder, and water in a medium saucepan. Bring to a boil, cover, and simmer for 20 to 25 minutes or until tender.

Remove the Tenders from the broth, and place in a shallow dish. Cover with the dressing and let stand for 20 minutes. Grill the Tenders for 3 to 5 minutes per side, basting liberally with the dressing. Remove from the grill and serve. You can also cut the Tenders into strips or chunks after grilling and serve on salad.

6 textured soy Chiken Tenders

1 to 2 tablespoons vegetarian chicken-flavored broth powder or equivalent

3 cups water

1 cup Italian dressing

Main Dishes

Per Serving: Calories 210, Protein 13 g, Soy Protein 13 g, Fat 13 g, Carbohydrates 8 g, Sodium 924 mg

# Smoky Mountain Barbecue Chiken Tenders

*Yield: 3 servings*

*Serve this on a bun to make an unforgetable barbecue sandwich.*

6 textured soy Chiken Tenders

1 to 2 tablespoons vegetarian chicken-flavored broth powder or equivalent

3 cups water

1 cup ketchup

4 tablespoons brown sugar

4 tablespoons sweetener

2 tablespoons yellow mustard

¼ cup water

2 tablespoons anchovy-free Worcestershire sauce

½ teaspoon minced fresh garlic

½ teaspoon Cajun seasoning

½ jalapeño, seeded and finely diced

1 tablespoon bourbon (optional)

Dash hickory smoke flavoring (optional)

Combine the Chiken Tenders, broth powder, and water in a medium saucepan. Bring to a boil, cover, and simmer for 20 to 25 minutes or until tender. While the Tenders are simmering, combine the remaining ingredients, and pour into a 9 x 9-inch baking dish.

Preheat the oven to 350°F. Place the Tenders in the baking dish, and smother with the sauce. Cover and bake for 20 minutes.

Main Dishes

Per Serving: Calories 273, Protein 14 g, Soy Protein 13 g, Fat 0 g, Carbohydrates 51 g, Sodium 1510 mg

# Johnny Cashew Chiken Tenders

*Yield: 3 servings*

*Add hot pepper sauce for a little kick.*

Combine the Chiken Tenders, broth powder, and water in a medium saucepan. Bring to a boil, cover, and simmer for 20 to 25 minutes or until tender.

While the Tenders are simmering, make a marinade by combining the remaining ingredients, except the cashews, in a shallow dish. Remove the Tenders from the broth, and place in the marinade. Cover and refrigerate for 1 to 2 hours.

Preheat the oven to 375°F. Remove the Tenders from the marinade, roll in the chopped cashews, and place on a oiled baking sheet. Bake for 20 minutes or until golden. Serve with sweet and sour sauce or hot mustard as a dipping sauce.

6 textured soy Chiken Tenders

1 to 2 tablespoons vegetarian chicken-flavored broth powder or equivalent

3 cups water

¼ cup sherry

2 tablespoons sesame oil

1 clove garlic, minced

2 tablespoons tamari or soy sauce

2 tablespoons sweetener

2 teaspoons minced fresh ginger

1½ cups finely chopped cashews

Main Dishes

Per Serving: Calories 659, Protein 25 g, Soy Protein 14 g, Fat 41 g, Carbohydrates 40 g, Sodium 902 mg

# Sweet-n-Spicy Chiken Tenders

Yield: 3 servings

*You can also serve on skewers for a great appetizer.*

6 textured soy Chiken Tenders

1 to 2 tablespoons vegetarian chicken-flavored broth powder or equivalent

3 cups water

1 white onion, chopped

1 green pepper, chopped

3 tablespoons ketchup

2 tablespoons fresh lemon juice

One 8-ounce can pineapple chunks with their juice

2 tablespoons soy sauce

1 teaspoon hot pepper sauce

½ teaspoon Cajun seasoning

1 tablespoon cornstarch

Combine the Chiken Tenders, broth powder, and water in a medium saucepan. Bring to a boil, cover, and simmer for 20 to 25 minutes or until tender.

While the Tenders are simmering, combine all the remaining ingredients, except the cornstarch, in a large skillet. Bring to a simmer and reduce the heat. Add the Tenders to the skillet, cover, and cook over low heat for 10 minutes. Mix the cornstarch with ¼ cup water, and add to the skillet. Continue to simmer and stir for 2 minutes. Add water if the sauce becomes too thick. Remove from the heat and serve.

Main Dishes

Per Serving: Calories 181, Protein 15 g, Soy Protein 14 g, Fat 0 g, Carbohydrates 28 g, Sodium 1049 mg

# Big Bayou Chiken Tenders

Yield: 3 servings

*A tablespoon of anchovy-free Worcestershire sauce adds a little zing to this.*

Combine the Chiken Tenders, broth powder, and water in a medium saucepan. Bring to a boil, cover, and simmer for 20 to 25 minutes or until tender.

While the Tenders are simmering, melt the margarine in a large saucepan over medium heat. Add the pecans and lightly brown. Add the remaining ingredients, except the Tenders, and simmer for 2 minutes. Remove the Tenders from the broth, and place in the pecan sauce. Simmer for 2 minutes and serve.

6 textured soy Chiken Tenders

1 to 2 tablespoons vegetarian chicken-flavored broth powder or equivalent

3 cups water

2 tablespoons dairy-free margarine

½ cup chopped pecans

¼ teaspoon Cajun seasoning

2 tablespoons brown sugar

1 teaspoon fresh lemon juice

¼ teaspoon grated lemon rind

¼ cup white wine

½ teaspoon hot pepper sauce

Main Dishes

Per Serving: Calories 305, Protein 15 g, Soy Protein 13 g, Fat 18 g, Carbohydrates 15 g, Sodium 311 mg

# Garlic Chiken Tenders

*Yield: 3 servings*

*Save any extra sauce for garlic bread.*

6 textured soy Chiken Tenders

1 to 2 tablespoons vegetarian chicken-flavored broth powder or equivalent

3 cups water

2 whole heads garlic, cloves separated and peeled

⅓ cup chopped celery

¾ cup dry white wine

¼ cup olive oil

2 tablespoons chopped fresh basil

2 tablespoons chopped fresh parsley

2 tablespoons fresh lemon juice

1 tablespoon fresh lime juice

½ teaspoon lemon zest

½ teaspoon ground peppercorns

Combine the Chiken Tenders, broth powder, and water in a medium saucepan. Bring to a boil, cover, and simmer for 20 to 25 minutes or until tender.

While the Chiken Tenders are simmering, preheat the oven to 375°F. Combine the remaining ingredients in a 9 x 9-inch baking dish, cover, and bake for 25 minutes. Remove the dish from the oven, and place the cooked Chiken Tenders in the garlic mixture, spooning the mixture over. Cover and bake for 15 minutes. Serve with crusty French or Italian bread.

Main Dishes

Per Serving: Calories 282, Protein 14 g, Soy Protein 13 g, Fat 16 g, Carbohydrates 7 g, Sodium 235 mg

# Spicy Maple Chiken Tenders

*Yield: 3 servings*

*Save any extra sauce for dipping.*

Combine the Chiken Tenders, broth powder, and water in a medium saucepan. Bring to a boil, cover, and simmer for 20 to 25 minutes or until tender.

Make a basting sauce by simmering the remaining ingredients in a medium saucepan for 2 to 3 minutes. Remove the Tenders from the broth, and dredge in the sauce. Place on a grill and cook for 3 to 4 minutes per side, basting with the sauce.

6 textured soy Chiken Tenders

I to 2 tablespoons vegetarian chicken-flavored broth powder or equivalent

3 cups water

¼ cup maple syrup

2 tablespoons chili sauce

I tablespoon vinegar

I tablespoon wasabi (Japanese horseradish)

I teaspoon mustard

Per Serving: Calories 160, Protein 13 g, Soy Protein 13 g, Fat 0 g, Carbohydrates 25 g, Sodium 401 mg

# Tortilla Crusted Chiken Tenders

*Yield: 3 servings*

*Salsa is excellent for dipping these succulent tenders into.*

6 textured soy Chiken Tenders

1 to 2 tablespoons vegetarian chicken-flavored broth powder or equivalent

3 cups water

⅓ cup canola oil

¼ cup chili powder

1 tablespoon finely chopped cilantro

½ teaspoon ground cumin

½ teaspoon oregano

½ teaspoon garlic powder

10 ounces white corn tortilla chips

Combine the Chiken Tenders, broth powder, and water in a medium saucepan. Bring to a boil, cover, and simmer for 20 to 25 minutes or until tender.

Preheat the oven to 375°F. Combine the oil, chili powder, cilantro, cumin, oregano, and garlic powder in a shallow bowl. Using a food processor or blender, crush the tortillas into a powder. Dip the Chiken Tenders in the flavored oil mixture, then dredge in the crushed tortillas. Place on a baking sheet, and bake for 25 minutes.

Main Dishes

Per Serving: Calories 743, Protein 20 g, Soy Protein 13 g, Fat 49 g, Carbohydrates 53 g, Sodium 223 mg

# Chiken Tenders Mole

*Yield: 3 servings*

*You can also chop up these tenders and use as a filling for tortillas.*

Combine the Chiken Tenders, broth powder, and water in a medium saucepan. Bring to a boil, cover, and simmer for 20 to 25 minutes or until tender.

While the Tenders are simmering, purée the remaining ingredients, except the chopped chocolate, in a blender until smooth. Pour this tomato mixture into a saucepan, and add the chocolate. Cover and simmer for about 5 minutes, then uncover and simmer for another 5 minutes, or until the mixture starts to thicken. Remove the Tenders from the broth, add to the sauce, and simmer for 2 minutes. Serve over rice.

6 textured soy Chiken Tenders

1 to 2 tablespoons vegetarian chicken-flavored broth powder or equivalent

3 cups water

2 tablespoons chili powder

½ teaspoon ground cinnamon

½ teaspoon ground black pepper

1 clove garlic, minced

One 14½-ounce can Mexican-style stewed tomatoes

½ cup prepared vegetarian chicken-flavored broth

½ ounce unsweetened baking chocolate, chopped

Main Dishes

Per Serving: Calories 153, Protein 15 g, Soy Protein 13 g, Fat 3 g, Carbohydrates 16 g, Sodium 293 mg

# Margarita Chiken Tenders

*Yield: 3 servings*

*Yellow rice compliments the spiciness of this dish.*

6 textured soy Chiken Tenders

1 to 2 tablespoons vegetarian chicken-flavored broth powder or equivalent

3 cups water

3 tablespoons fresh lime juice

2 tablespoons canola oil

2 tablespoons sweetener

1 tablespoon orange juice

1 teaspoon grated lime zest

2 tablespoons finely chopped cilantro

1 teaspoon minced, seeded jalapeño

Combine the Chiken Tenders, broth powder, and water in a medium saucepan. Bring to a boil, cover, and simmer for 20 to 25 minutes or until tender.

While the Tenders are simmering, make a marinade by combining the remaining ingredients in a shallow bowl. Remove the Tenders from the broth, place in the marinade, and let stand for 15 minutes. Grill the Tenders for 3 to 5 minutes per side, basting liberally with the marinade. Serve with the remaining marinade.

Per Serving: Calories 193, Protein 13 g, Soy Protein 13 g, Fat 9 g, Carbohydrates 14 g, Sodium 234 mg

# Grilled Chiken Tenders with Papaya Salsa

*Yield: 3 servings*

*Slice these tenders and serve with mixed greens for a salad.*

Combine the Chiken Tenders, broth powder, and water in a medium saucepan. Bring to a boil, cover, and simmer for 20 to 25 minutes or until tender.

While the Tenders are simmering, make a fresh salsa by chopping the remaining ingredients in a blender until just mixed. Remove the Tenders from the broth, and place in a shallow dish. Cover with the salsa and let stand for 15 minutes. Place the Tenders on a grill, and cook for 3 to 5 minutes per side. Remove from the grill, top with the remaining salsa, and serve.

6 textured soy Chiken Tenders

1 to 2 tablespoons vegetarian chicken-flavored broth powder or equivalent

3 cups water

½ papaya

½ apple

½ red onion

½ jalapeño, seeded

2 cloves garlic

2 tablespoons chopped fresh cilantro

1 tablespoon lime juice

1 tablespoon canola oil

Main Dishes

Per Serving: Calories 160, Protein 14 g, Soy Protein 13 g, Fat 4 g, Carbohydrates 14 g, Sodium 243 mg

# Chiken Tenders Satay with Spicy Peanut Sauce

*Yield: 6 servings*

*Double the sauce to make extra for dipping.*

6 textured soy Chiken Tenders

1 to 2 tablespoons vegetarian chicken-flavored broth powder or equivalent

3 cups water

⅓ cup creamy peanut butter

3 tablespoons coconut milk

3 tablespoons soy sauce

2 tablespoons lime juice

1 tablespoon vegetable oil

2 cloves garlic

2 green onions

½ teaspoon hot pepper sauce

Combine the Chiken Tenders, broth powder, and water in a medium saucepan. Bring to a boil, cover, and simmer for 20 to 25 minutes or until tender.

Make a peanut sauce by processing the remaining ingredients in a blender until smooth. Pour into a small bowl. Remove the Tenders from the broth, and dip in the peanut sauce. Place on metal or bamboo skewers, and grill for 3 minutes on each side. Serve with the remaining sauce.

Main Dishes

Per Serving: Calories 162, Protein 11 g, Soy Protein 14 g, Fat 10 g, Carbohydrates 6 g, Sodium 618 mg

# Grilled Szechuan Chiken Skewers

*Yield: 6 servings*

*Sweet and sour sauce or hot mustard sauce are great for dipping these tenders.*

Combine the Chiken Tenders, broth powder, and water in a medium saucepan. Bring to a boil, cover, and simmer for 20 to 25 minutes or until tender.

Make a marinade by combining the remaining ingredients in a shallow bowl, and mix well. Remove the Tenders from the broth, place in the marinade, and let stand for 15 to 30 minutes. Place on metal or bamboo skewers, and grill for 3 minutes on each side, basting with the remaining sauce. Serve with rice.

6 textured soy Chiken Tenders

1 to 2 tablespoons vegetarian chicken-flavored broth powder or equivalent

3 cups water

2 tablespoons orange juice

2 tablespoons soy sauce

2 teaspoons minced fresh ginger

1 teaspoon orange zest

½ teaspoon crushed red pepper

1 clove garlic, minced

½ teaspoon sugar

Per Serving: Calories 46, Protein 7 g, Soy Protein 14 g, Fat 0 g, Carbohydrates 3 g, Sodium 445 mg

Main Dishes

# Tandoori Style Chiken Tenders

*Yield: 3 servings*

*Basmati rice makes a nice side dish.*

6 textured soy Chiken Tenders

1 to 2 tablespoons vegetarian chicken-flavored broth powder or equivalent

3 cups water

1 cup plain soy yogurt

2 teaspoons curry powder

2 tablespoons lemon juice

½ teaspoon salt

1 clove garlic, minced

1 teaspoon paprika

½ teaspoon cardamom

½ teaspoon ginger

¼ teaspoon cayenne pepper

Combine the Chiken Tenders, broth powder, and water in a medium saucepan. Bring to a boil, cover, and simmer for 20 to 25 minutes or until tender.

While the Tenders are simmering, make a marinade by combining the remaining ingredients in a shallow bowl. Remove the Tenders from the broth, and place in the marinade. Cover and refrigerate for a minimum of 2 hours. (Overnight is better.) Grill for 4 to 5 minutes per side, basting liberally with the marinade. Serve over rice.

Main Dishes

Per Serving: Calories 106, Protein 15 g, Soy Protein 17 g, Fat 1 g, Carbohydrates 7 g, Sodium 585 mg

# Chiken Tenders Sake Style

*Yield: 3 servings*

*Serve with wasabi and soy sauce on the side.*

Combine the Chiken Tenders, broth powder, and water in a medium saucepan. Bring to a boil, cover, and simmer for 20 to 25 minutes or until tender.

Make a marinade by combining the remaining ingredients in a shallow dish. Remove the Tenders from the broth, and place in the marinade. Cover and refrigerate for 30 minutes. Grill the Tenders for 3 to 5 minutes per side, basting liberally with the marinade. Serve with rice.

6 textured soy Chiken Tenders

1 to 2 tablespoons vegetarian chicken-flavored broth powder or equivalent

3 cups water

¼ cup soy sauce

¼ cup sake, dry sherry, or nonalcoholic white wine

¼ cup prepared vegetarian chicken-flavored broth

1 tablespoon sweetener

½ teaspoon ginger

1 teaspoon minced fresh garlic

Dash hot pepper sauce

Main Dishes

Per Serving: Calories 131, Protein 16 g, Soy Protein 15 g, Fat 0 g, Carbohydrates 11 g, Sodium 1561 mg

# Good Ol' Chiken Nuggets

*Yield: 4 servings*

*Barbecue or hot mustard sauces are perfect for dipping.*

I cup textured soy Chopped Chiken

1 1/2 cups water

I to 2 tablespoons vegetarian chicken-flavored broth powder or equivalent

I cup flake cereal crumbs

1/4 cup flour

1 1/2 teaspoons vegetarian chicken-flavored broth powder or equivalent

1/2 teaspoon Cajun seasoning

Combine the Chopped Chiken, water, and broth powder in a medium saucepan. Bring to a boil, cover, and simmer for 15 minutes or until tender.

Preheat the oven to 400°F. Combine the remaining ingredients in a paper bag. Remove several pieces of the cooked Chopped Chiken pieces from the saucepan, and place in the bag. Shake to coat, then place on a greased baking sheet. Continue with the other pieces until all are coated. Bake for 15 minutes and serve with your favorite dipping sauces.

Per Serving: Calories 161, Protein 12 g, Soy Protein 9 g, Fat 0 g, Carbohydrates 28 g, Sodium 439 mg

# Appalachian Stew

*Yield: 8 servings*

*Great on a wintery night with fresh baked bread.*

Combine all the ingredients in a large stockpot, and bring to a boil. Reduce the heat, cover, and simmer for ½ hour. Remove the lid and continue cooking for 1 hour, or until the liquid has thickened and the vegetables are tender.

1 cup textured soy Chopped Chiken

2 quarts water

3 tablespoons vegetarian chicken-flavored broth powder or equivalent

One 10-ounce package frozen lima beans

1 large potato, cubed

1 large onion, chopped

2 celery stalks, chopped

½ cup sliced carrots

One 16-ounce can stewed tomatoes

One 16-ounce can whole kernel corn

1 teaspoon cayenne pepper

2 cloves garlic, minced

1 teaspoon chili powder

1½ ounces bourbon (optional)

2 tablespoons anchovy-free Worcestershire sauce

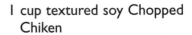

Main Dishes

Per Serving: Calories 165, Protein 9 g, Soy Protein 5 g, Fat 0 g, Carbohydrates 30 g, Sodium 327 mg

# South American Chiken Stew

*Yield: 8 servings*

*This is also great as a filling for tortillas.*

1 cup textured soy Chopped Chiken

1½ cups water

1 to 2 tablespoons vegetarian chicken-flavored broth powder or equivalent

1 white onion, chopped

2 celery ribs, chopped

1 clove garlic, minced

2 tablespoons canola oil

One 10-ounce can condensed tomato soup

½ teaspoon chili powder

½ teaspoon nutmeg

¼ teaspoon cinnamon

2½ cups shredded potatoes

⅔ cup shredded carrots

⅓ cup orange juice

½ teaspoon salt

Dash ground pepper

Combine the Chopped Chiken, water, and broth powder in a medium saucepan. Bring to a boil, cover, and simmer for 15 minutes or until tender.

In a large skillet, sauté the onion, celery, and garlic in the oil for 3 to 5 minutes over medium-high heat. Add the condensed soup, chili powder, nutmeg, and cinnamon, and bring to a boil, then remove from the heat and set aside.

Preheat the oven to 400°F. Add the Chopped Chiken, potatoes, carrots, orange juice, salt, and pepper to the skillet, and combine with the soup mixture. Pour into a greased 2-inch-deep baking dish. Cover and bake for 30 minutes.

Main Dishes

Per Serving: Calories 141, Protein 6 g, Soy Protein 5 g, Fat 3 g, Carbohydrates 20 g, Sodium 505 mg

# Chiken Pilaf

*Yield: 4 servings*

*Substitute cilantro for the parsley for a Southwestern flair.*

Combine the Chopped Chiken, water, and broth powder in a medium saucepan. Bring to a boil, cover, and simmer for 15 minutes or until tender.

In a large stockpot, sauté the onion, celery, carrot, and garlic in the oil until soft. Add ¼ cup of the prepared broth over medium-high heat, cover, and simmer for 5 minutes. Add the cooked Chopped Chiken, remaining broth, and rice. Cover and simmer over low to medium heat for 15 minutes. Add the parsley, salt, pepper, soymilk, and tomato paste, and simmer uncovered for 5 minutes. Remove from the heat and serve.

1 cup textured soy Chopped Chiken

1½ cups water

1 to 2 tablespoons vegetarian chicken-flavored broth powder or equivalent

1 small white onion, chopped

1 celery rib, chopped

1 carrot, peeled and sliced

1 clove garlic, minced

2 tablespoons canola oil

2 cups prepared vegetarian chicken-flavored broth

1½ cups long grain rice

2 tablespoons chopped parsley

1 teaspoon salt

½ teaspoon pepper

½ cup plain soymilk

2 tablespoons tomato paste

Main Dishes

Per Serving: Calories 288, Protein 14 g, Soy Protein 10 g, Fat 7 g, Carbohydrates 39 g, Sodium 862 mg

# Chili Verde Style

*Yield: 6 servings*

*Use stewed tomatillos instead of the tomatoes for an even greener chili.*

1 cup textured soy Chopped Chiken

1½ cups water

1 to 2 tablespoons vegetarian chicken-flavored broth powder or equivalent

1 large white onion, chopped

2 cloves garlic, minced

2 tablespoons canola oil

One 14-ounce can stewed tomatoes

One 4-ounce can green chiles

1 tablespoon chili powder

1½ teaspoons cumin

1 cup prepared vegetarian chicken-flavored broth

2 tablespoons fresh chopped cilantro

Combine the Chopped Chiken, water, and broth powder in a medium saucepan. Bring to a boil, cover, and simmer for 15 minutes or until tender.

In a medium skillet, sauté the onion and garlic in the oil over medium-high heat for 3 to 5 minutes. Add the remaining ingredients, except the cilantro, to the skillet, and bring to a low boil. Add the cooked Chopped Chiken, cover, and simmer for 20 minutes. Add the cilantro and cook uncovered for 5 to 10 minutes, or until the sauce begins to thicken. Serve with rice or tortillas.

Main Dishes

Per Serving: Calories 129, Protein 12 g, Soy Protein 6 g, Fat 0 g, Carbohydrates 21 g, Sodium 160 mg

# Chiken Japanese Steakhouse Style

*Yield: 4 servings*

*Double the sauce if you like extra for dipping.*

Combine the Chopped Chiken, water, and broth powder in a medium saucepan. Bring to a boil, cover, and simmer for 15 minutes or until tender. Process all the remaining ingredients, except the green onion and canola oil, in a blender until combined.

In a medium skillet, sauté the cooked Chopped Chiken and green onion in the oil for 1 minute. Add the blended sauce and simmer over medium-high heat for 3 to 5 minutes. Serve with rice and spoon extra sauce over each serving.

1 cup textured soy Chopped Chiken

1½ cups water

1 to 2 tablespoons vegetarian chicken-flavored broth powder or equivalent

⅓ cup soy sauce

2 tablespoons sweetener

2 cloves garlic

2 tablespoons dry mustard

1 teaspoon grated fresh ginger

1 teaspoon lemon juice

2 tablespoons sesame seeds

2 green onions, chopped

2 tablespoons canola oil

Per Serving: Calories 174, Protein 12 g, Soy Protein 11 g, Fat 9 g, Carbohydrates 11 g, Sodium 1422 mg

Main Dishes

# Far East Chiken

*Yield: 4 servings*

*White or fried rice is the traditional accompaniment for this dish.*

1 cup textured soy Chopped Chiken

1½ cups water

1 to 2 tablespoons vegetarian chicken-flavored broth powder or equivalent

2 tablespoons soy sauce

2 tablespoons lemon juice

2 tablespoons sweetener

1 clove garlic, minced

1 teaspoon grated fresh ginger,

2 teaspoons cornstarch

½ teaspoon hot pepper sauce

¼ cup prepared vegetarian chicken-flavored broth

8 ounces snow peas

1 red bell pepper, sliced

2 green onions, sliced

1 apple, peeled, cored, and sliced

Combine the Chopped Chiken, water, and broth powder in a medium saucepan. Bring to a boil, cover, and simmer for 15 minutes or until tender. Process the soy sauce, lemon juice, sweetener, garlic, ginger, cornstarch, and hot pepper sauce in a blender until mixed.

In a medium skillet, bring the prepared broth to a simmer over medium-high heat. Add the snow peas and bell pepper, and cook for 2 to 3 minutes. Reduce the heat and add the Chopped Chiken, green onions, apple, and blended sauce. Cook, stirring frequently, for 3 to 5 minutes, or until the sauce thickens.

Main Dishes

Per Serving: Calories 129, Protein 12 g, Soy Protein 10 g, Fat 0 g, Carbohydrates 21 g, Sodium 570 mg

# Marengo Chiken

Yield: 4 servings

*For a heartier dish, serve over pasta.*

Combine the Chopped Chiken, water, and broth powder in a medium saucepan. Bring to a boil, cover, and simmer for 15 minutes or until tender.

In large stock pot, sauté the onions, mushrooms, and garlic in the oil over medium-high heat for 5 minutes. Add the cooked Chopped Chiken, parsley, and thyme, and cook for 1 minute. Add the tomatoes and juice, wine, and tomato paste, and simmer for 25 minutes, or until the liquid begins to thicken. Add salt and pepper to taste, and serve.

1 cup textured soy Chopped Chiken

1½ cups water

1 to 2 tablespoons vegetarian chicken-flavored broth powder or equivalent

1 white onion, chopped

1 cup sliced mushrooms

2 cloves garlic, minced

2 tablespoons olive oil

2 tablespoons chopped fresh parsley

½ teaspoon dried thyme

One 14-ounce can diced plum tomatoes with their juice

⅓ cup white wine

2 tablespoons tomato paste

Salt and pepper, to taste

Main Dishes

Per Serving: Calories 164, Protein 11 g, Soy Protein 7 g, Fat 7 g, Carbohydrates 11 g, Sodium 182 mg

# Sloppy Joes

*Increase the hot pepper sauce for extra spicy Joes.*

1½ cups water

2 teaspoons vegetarian ham-flavored broth powder

1½ cups textured soy "Pork" Strips

⅓ cup chopped onion

⅓ cup chopped green pepper

2 tablespoons canola oil

One 8-ounce can tomato sauce

2 tablespoons quick oats

1 teaspoon chili powder

1 teaspoon brown sugar

1 teaspoon anchovy-free Worcestershire sauce

½ teaspoon garlic salt

Dash hot pepper sauce

6 sandwich buns

In a medium saucepan, bring the water to boil. Add the broth powder and mix well. Stir in the "Pork" Strips, and simmer for 5 minutes. Remove from the heat and let cool.

Chop the cooked "Pork" Strips into ¼-inch bits. In a medium skillet, sauté the onion and green pepper in the canola oil over medium-high heat until tender. Add the chopped "Pork" Strips and remaining ingredients (except the buns) to the skillet, bring to a boil, reduce the heat, and simmer for 3 to 5 minutes. Remove the sloppy joe mixture from the heat, and serve on the buns.

Main Dishes

Per Serving: Calories 208, Protein 10 g, Soy Protein 5 g, Fat 6 g, Carbohydrates 28 g, Sodium 709 mg

# Southern "Pork" Barbecue

*Yield: 4 servings*

*For a great sandwich, serve this in a whole grain bun, topped with coleslaw and pickles.*

In a medium saucepan, combine all the ingredients, except the "Pork" Strips. Bring the mixture to a boil, then reduce the heat and simmer. Add the "Pork" Strips and let simmer for 10 minutes.

Preheat the oven to 350°F. Place the mixture into a 9 x 9-inch baking dish, cover, and bake for 20 minutes. Serve with bread or potato salad.

1 cup ketchup

½ cup chopped white onions

¼ cup brown sugar

¼ cup sweetener

¼ cup water

2 tablespoons yellow mustard

2 tablespoons anchovy-free Worcestershire sauce

½ teaspoon minced garlic

½ teaspoon Cajun seasoning

½ jalapeño, seeded and finely diced (optional)

1 cup textured soy "Pork" Strips

Per Serving: Calories 178, Protein 6 g, Soy Protein 5 g, Fat 0 g, Carbohydrates 38 g, Sodium 717 mg

Main Dishes

# Red Beans & Rice

*Yield: 4 servings*

*Keep an extra bottle of hot pepper sauce on the table for this dish.*

1 cup textured soy "Pork" Strips

1½ cups water

1 teaspoon vegetarian ham-flavored broth powder

Two 14½-ounce cans red or kidney beans

½ cup chopped white onion

2 cloves garlic, minced

1 bay leaf

1 teaspoon Cajun seasoning

1 teaspoon hot pepper sauce

2 cups hot cooked white rice

Combine all the ingredients, except the rice, in a large saucepan. Cover and simmer for 15 to 20 minutes. Uncover and continue cooking to thicken the sauce, or add water to thin the sauce. Remove from the heat after reaching the desired thickness, discard the bay leaf, and serve over the rice.

Main Dishes

Per Serving: Calories 376, Protein 22 g, Soy Protein 5 g, Fat 1 g, Carbohydrates 68 g, Sodium 43 mg

# Carnitas

*Yield: 6 servings*

*Cilantro makes a nice topping for this traditional Mexican dish.*

Combine all the ingredients in a large pot, and bring to a boil. Reduce the heat, cover, and simmer for 25 minutes. Discard the bay leaf, and serve as a filling in tortillas. Top with salsa, if desired.

2 cups textured soy "Pork" Strips

2 cups water

2 teaspoons vegetarian ham-flavored broth powder

3 cloves garlic, chopped

¼ cup chopped white onion

⅓ cup dry white wine

½ teaspoon dried oregano

I bay leaf

½ teapoon ground pepper.

Per Serving: Calories 48, Protein 7 g, Soy Protein 7 g, Fat 0 g, Carbohydrates 3 g, Sodium 51 mg

# Spanish Rice

*Add corn and green peas for a colorful combination.*

1 cup water

2 teaspoons vegetarian beef-flavored broth powder or equivalent

1 cup beef-style textured soy protein granules

3 tablespoons vegetable oil

1 cup rice

½ cup chopped onion

1 clove garlic, minced

½ cup chopped green bell pepper

2½ cups diced canned tomatoes (two 14½-ounce cans)

2 teaspoons chili powder

In a small saucepan, bring the water to a boil. Add the broth powder and textured soy granules. Mix well, remove from the heat, and let stand for 10 minutes.

Heat the oil in large nonstick skillet, and add the rice. Sauté, stirring constantly, until lightly browned, about 10 minutes. Add the onion, garlic, green peppers, and soy granules. Cook until the onion is limp and lightly browned, stirring often to break up and brown the granules. Add the undrained diced tomatoes and chili powder. Cover and simmer about 25 minutes, or until the rice is tender and most of the liquid has been absorbed. Cover and let stand about 5 minutes before serving.

NOTE: If the rice sticks to the pan, add more water as necessary.

Main Dishes

Per Serving: Calories 251, Protein 12 g, Soy Protein 7 g, Fat 8 g, Carbohydrates 40 g, Sodium 466 mg

# Southern Dressing

*Yield: 6 servings*

*Serve with cranberry sauce and roasted vegetables for a holiday meal.*

2 cups unflavored textured soy protein granules

4 cups water

3 tablespoons vegetarian chicken-flavored broth powder or equivalent

1 cup chopped onions

1 cup chopped celery

¼ cup diced green bell peppers

¼ cup dairy-free margarine

1 tablespoon flour

⅛ teaspoon pepper

In a medium saucepan, bring the water to a boil, add the broth powder, and mix well. Remove 2 cups of the broth, and set aside. Add the textured soy granules to the remaining broth in the saucepan, and set aside for 10 minutes

Sauté the onion, celery, and green peppers in the ¼ cup margarine until tender; the onion should be translucent and limp. Blend in the 1 tablespoon flour and pepper. Add the granules and mix gently. Place this mixture in a deep, 2-quart baking dish.

Prepare the topping by combining the 1 cup flour, cornmeal, baking powder, sugar, sage, thyme, and pepper in a small mixing bowl. Cut in the shortening. Combine the egg replacer and milk, and add to the flour mixture. Blend well.

Preheat the oven to 350° F. Spoon the topping over the textured soy mixture. Bring the reserved 2 cups broth to a boil, and slowly pour over the topping. Place the casserole in the

Main Dishes

*Topping*

1 cup flour

½ cup cornmeal

1 tablespoon baking powder

2 teaspoons sugar

¼ teaspoon ground sage

¼ teaspoon ground thyme

⅛ teaspoon pepper

1 tablespoon vegetable shortening

Egg replacer equivalent to 3 eggs

¾ cup nondairy milk

½ cup nondairy shredded cheese (optional)

oven, and bake for 40 to 45 minutes, or until golden brown. Sprinkle a little shredded cheese over the topping for the last 5 minutes of cooking time, if desired. Let stand 10 minutes before serving.

Per Serving: Calories 316, Protein 21 g, Soy Protein 13 g, Fat 8 g, Carbohydrates 44 g, Sodium 670 mg

# Fried Rice

*Yield: 6 servings*

*To save time, chop all the vegetables for this recipe first, and set aside.*

In a small saucepan, bring the water to a boil. Add the broth powder and textured soy granules, mix well, and let stand 10 minutes.

Heat the oil in a large nonstick skillet over medium-high heat. Add the onions and garlic, and sauté until golden. Add the textured soy protein, and cook 1 minute. Add the celery, carrot, red bell pepper, and peas, and stir-fry for 3 minutes. Add the water chestnuts, sunflower seeds, green onions, bacon-flavored bits, and rice, and stir-fry for 3 minutes, or until the rice is hot. Add the soy sauce, sugar, and pepper, and cook, stirring constantly, until the sauce is mixed thoroughly.

½ cup water

I teaspoon vegetarian chicken-flavored broth powder or equivalent

½ cup unflavored textured soy protein granules

3 tablespoons oil

½ cup chopped onion

I clove garlic, minced

¼ cup chopped celery

I carrot, grated

¼ cup chopped red bell pepper

I cup frozen peas, thawed

One-half 8-ounce can water chestnuts, chopped

¼ cup sunflower seeds

¼ cup chopped green onions

3 tablespoons bacon-flavored soy bits

3 cups rice, cooked and chilled to keep the grains separate

¼ cup soy sauce

I tablespoon sugar

½ teaspoon pepper

Per Serving: Calories 315, Protein 11 g, Soy Protein 5 g, Fat 11 g, Carbohydrates 43 g, Sodium 791 mg

Main Dishes

# I Can't Believe
# It's Not Meat!

# Soups

# Oriental Vegetable Soup

Yield: 10 servings

*Oriental rice crackers are good with this soup; they are usually available in the Asian food section at the grocery.*

2 tablespoons dairy-free margarine

1½ cups chopped onions

1½ cups chopped carrots

1½ cups chopped celery

1 teaspoon curry powder

10 cups water

1 tart apple, chopped

¼ teaspoon pepper

3 tablespoons vegetarian chicken-flavored broth powder or equivalent

1½ cups pasta shells

1 cup unflavored textured soy protein granules

One 10-ounce package frozen corn

One 10-ounce package frozen lima beans

2 tablespoons chopped fresh parsley

Melt the margarine in a 5-quart kettle or pot. Sauté the onions, carrots, celery, and curry powder over medium heat until the onions are tender and limp, about 5 minutes. Add the water, apple, pepper, and broth powder, bring to a boil, then reduce the heat. Cover and simmer for 30 minutes or until the carrots are tender, stirring occasionally. Cook the pasta and set aside.

Add the textured soy granules, corn, and lima beans to the broth mixture, and cook for 30 minutes longer. Add the pasta to the soup, remove from the heat, cover, and let stand for about 10 minutes before serving. Sprinkle the top with chopped parsley, and serve.

Per Serving: Calories 199, Protein 11 g, Soy Protein 4 g, Fat 4 g, Carbohydrates 34 g, Sodium 347 mg

# Thai Chiken Breast and Ginger-Coconut Soup

*Yield: 6 servings*

*Try serving this over a small amount of white rice.*

Combine all the ingredients, except the cilantro and green onion, in a large saucepan. Bring to a boil, cover, and simmer for 35 minutes.

Remove the Chiken Breasts and slice into ¼-inch strips. Add the Breast strips back to the soup, along with the cilantro and green onion, and serve.

4 textured soy Chiken Breasts

6 cups prepared vegetarian chicken-flavored broth

One 14-ounce can coconut milk

¼ cup sliced mushrooms

2 tablespoons grated fresh ginger

2 tablespoons lime juice

½ tablespoon grated lemon zest

1 teaspoon garlic powder

1 teaspoon hot pepper sauce

¼ cup chopped cilantro

2 tablespoons sliced green onion

Soups

Per Serving: Calories 216, Protein 9 g, Soy Protein 7 g, Fat 16 g, Carbohydrates 7 g, Sodium 302 mg

# Chiken Breast-Corn Tortilla Soup

*Yield: 6 servings*

*Be sure and serve this with extra cilantro and tortillas for garnish.*

4 textured soy Chiken Breasts

I to 2 tablespoons vegetarian chicken-flavored broth powder or equivalent

3 cups water

3 tablespoons olive oil

I corn tortilla, cut into I-inch strips

2 cloves garlic, minced

2 tablespoons minced onion

½ small jalapeño, seeded and minced

One 16-ounce can yellow or white corn

One 16-ounce can chopped tomatoes

¼ cup tomato paste

2 teaspoons cumin

½ tablespoon salt

½ teaspoon chili powder

I teaspoon lime juice

2 cups water

4 cups prepared vegetarian chicken-flavored broth

I bunch cilantro, chopped

Tortilla chips

Combine the Chiken Breasts, broth powder, and water in a medium saucepan. Bring to a boil, cover, and simmer for 35 to 40 minutes or until tender.

While the Breasts are simmering, heat the tortilla strips in the olive oil in a medium skillet over medium-high heat until golden and crisp. Add the garlic, onion, and jalapeño to the skillet, and cook for about 2 minutes, or until the onion is tender.

In a blender, combine ½ of the corn and the remaining ingredients, except the broth, cilantro and tortilla chips. Add the tortilla mixture to the blender, and mix until combined. Pour the contents of the blender back into a medium saucepan, and bring to a simmer over medium heat. Remove the Chiken Breasts from the hot broth, and cut into ¼-inch strips. Add to the soup along with the broth and remaining corn, and simmer for 5 minutes. Serve with the cilantro and tortilla chips as garnishes.

Per Serving: Calories 205, Protein 10 g, Soy Protein 7 g, Fat 7 g, Carbohydrates 23 g, Sodium 854 mg

# Mexican Corn Chowder

*Yield: 6 servings*

*Serve this soup with jalapeño or chile corn bread.*

Combine all the ingredients, except the textured soy strips, in a large saucepan. Bring the mixture to a boil, reduce the heat to simmer, and add the textured soy strips. Cover and cook over medium-low heat for 45 minutes. Serve as a soup with tortilla chips or crackers.

Two 14½-ounce cans stewed tomatoes

2 cups water

3 tablespoons vegetarian beef-flavored broth powder or equivalent

1 tablespoon chili powder

1 teaspoon cumin

½ teaspoon paprika

½ teaspoon pepper

1 jalapeño, seeded and chopped

1 cup frozen corn kernels

2 carrots, sliced

One 15-ounce can black beans, drained

2 potatoes, peeled and cubed

½ yellow bell pepper, chopped

¼ cup finely chopped cilantro

2 tablespoons sweetener

⅓ cup fresh orange juice

1 cup beef-style textured soy protein strips

Soups

Per Serving: Calories 344, Protein 20 g, Soy Protein 5 g, Fat 3 g, Carbohydrates 71 g, Sodium 656 mg

# Chiken Chili Stew

Yield: 6 servings

*Adding minced jalapeño makes an extra spicy chili.*

1 cup textured soy Chopped Chiken

1½ cups water

1 to 2 tablespoons vegetarian chicken-flavored broth powder or equivalent

1 cup tomato sauce

One 14-ounce can stewed tomatoes

1 cup prepared vegetarian chicken-flavored broth

1 large white onion, chopped

3 cloves garlic, minced

2 tablespoons canola oil

¼ cup chili powder

1 teaspoon oregano

½ teaspoon cayenne pepper

½ teaspoon cinnamon

2 tablespoons grated semi-sweet chocolate

1 teaspoon cumin

½ teaspoon black pepper

2 tablespoons chopped fresh cilantro

Combine the Chopped Chiken, water, and broth powder in a medium saucepan. Bring to a boil, cover, and simmer for 15 minutes or until tender.

In a large stock pot, sauté the onion and garlic in the oil over medium-high heat for 3 to 5 minutes. Add the remaining ingredients (except the cilantro) to the stock pot, and bring to a low boil. Try to break up the tomatoes into smaller pieces as they cook. Cover and simmer for 30 to 45 minutes, or until the stock begins to thicken. Add the fresh cilantro and serve.

Per Serving: Calories 141, Protein 8 g, Soy Protein 6 g, Fat 6 g, Carbohydrates 12 g, Sodium 406 mg

# I Can't Believe It's Not Meat!

# Salads

# Vegetarian Chicken Salad Spread

*Yield: 6 servings*

*Wrap this up in lettuce leaves for a unique luncheon dish.*

½ cup water

½ cup unflavored textured soy protein granules

2 teaspoons vegetarian chicken-flavored broth powder or equivalent

3 tablespoons dairy-free mayonnaise

2 tablespoons soy sour cream

2 tablespoons chopped green onions

2 tablespoons chopped nuts

¼ teaspoon curry powder

In a small saucepan, bring the water to a boil, then add the textured soy granules and broth powder. Remove from the heat, mix well, and let cool. In a mixing bowl, combine all the ingredients, and mix thoroughly. Serve on bread, crackers, or pita bread.

Per Serving: Calories 88, Protein 5 g, Soy Protein 4 g, Fat 6 g, Carbohydrates 5 g, Sodium 94 mg

# California Pasta Salad

Yield: 8 servings

*A summer favorite that is quick and easy; this large recipe will disappear quickly.*

In a small saucepan, bring the water to a boil. Add the broth powder and mix well. Stir in the textured soy granules, remove from the heat, and let cool.

Cook the macaroni according to the package instructions. Drain and cool.

In a a medium bowl, combine the tomatoes, jalapeños, red onion, garlic, lemon juice, and cilantro. Mix well and set aside. Peel and dice the avocados.

In a serving bowl, combine 2½ cups of the tomato mixture, the textured soy granules, and diced avocados. Gently stir in the cooled pasta. Serve any remaining tomato mixture with baked tortilla chips as a side dish.

1 cup water

4 teaspoons vegetarian chicken-flavored broth powder or equivalent

1 cup unflavored textured soy protein granules

1 pound macaroni

4 large tomatoes, finely chopped

1 tablespoon seeded, chopped jalapeño

1 small red onion, finely chopped

1 clove garlic, minced

1 teaspoon lemon juice

2 tablespoons finely chopped cilantro

2 medium avocados

Salads

Per Serving: Calories 328, Protein 15 g, Soy Protein 5 g, Fat 7 g, Carbohydrates 54 g, Sodium 109 mg

# Spicy Pasta Salad

*Yield: 8 servings*

*Other fresh vegetables may be added, such as chopped tomatoes, thinly sliced zucchini, and sliced yellow squash.*

1 cup water

4 teaspoons vegetarian chicken-flavored broth powder or equivalent

1 cup unflavored textured soy protein granules

1 pound linguini

½ cup dairy-free mayonnaise

1 small clove garlic, minced

1 teaspoon chopped pimiento

⅛ teaspoon pepper

Dash cayenne pepper

2 tablespoons sodium-free Italian salad dressing

1 red bell pepper

4 green onions, thinly sliced

2 tablespoons dried parsley

2 tablespoons drained capers

In a small saucepan, bring the water to a boil. Add the broth powder and mix well. Stir in the textured soy granules, remove from the heat, and let cool.

Cook the linguini according to the package instructions, then rinse and cool.

Combine the mayonnaise, garlic, pimiento, pepper, cayenne pepper, and Italian salad dressing; set aside.

Cut the red bell pepper in half, and broil skin side up 6 inches from the heat element until blackened. Place the pepper in a paper bag, and let cool for 10 minutes. (The pepper will steam in its own heat, causing the skin to separate from the flesh easily.) Remove the skin, seeds, and ribs of the pepper, then dice and set aside.

In a large bowl, combine the textured soy granules, red pepper, green onions, parsley, capers, and mayonnaise mixture. Gently combine the with pasta, and toss.

Per Serving: Calories 360, Protein 15 g, Soy Protein 5 g, Fat 10 g, Carbohydrates 55 g, Sodium 183 mg

# Santa Cruz Salad

*Yield: 4 servings*

*Try on a bed of lettuce or as a filling for pita bread.*

In a medium saucepan, bring the water to a boil. Add the broth powder and mix well. Stir in the textured soy granules, remove from the heat, and let cool. After the granules have cooled, combine with the remaining ingredients. Add more mayonnaise if desired. Chill for 1 hour and serve.

2 cups water

3 tablespoons vegetarian chicken-flavored broth powder or equivalent

2 cups unflavored textured soy protein granules

½ cup shredded soy Monterey Jack

½ cup shredded soy cheddar

I avocado, diced

½ cup chopped olives

I small tomato, chopped

I teaspoon chopped onions

I teaspoon minced green chiles

½ teaspoon chili powder

¼ teaspoon garlic powder

Dash of pepper

¼ cup dairy-free mayonnaise

Salads

Per Serving: Calories 339, Protein 33 g, Soy Protein 28 g, Fat 15 g, Carbohydrates 24 g, Sodium 775 mg

# Curried Beef-Style Salad

*Yield: 6 servings*

*Pita chips can be mixed into this salad.*

1 cup beef-style textured soy protein strips

½ cup water

2 teaspoons vegetarian beef-flavored broth powder or equivalent

1 cup canned green beans, drained

2 tablespoons dried parsley

1 apple, chopped

1 stalk celery, chopped

3 green onions, chopped

2 ounces pimiento, chopped

½ cup long-grain cooked rice

*Dressing*

½ cup canola oil

½ cup red wine vinegar

2 tablespoons Dijon mustard

2 teaspoons curry powder

⅛ teaspoon pepper

2 tablespoons sweetener

To make the dressing, mix the oil, red wine vinegar, Dijon mustard, curry powder, pepper, and sweetener in a small bowl.

In a medium saucepan, combine the textured soy strips, water, broth powder, and ½ cup of the dressing mixture. Bring barely to a boil, and simmer for 15 minutes. Remove from the heat, drain the excess liquid, and let cool.

In a large mixing bowl, add the green beans, parsley, apple, celery, green onions, pimiento, and rice. Add the cooled textured soy strips and remaining dressing to the vegetable mixture. Toss lightly and serve.

Per Serving: Calories 322, Protein 10 g, Soy Protein 5 g, Fat 19 g, Carbohydrates 35 g, Sodium 312 mg

# Waldorf Salad With Shredded Chiken Breasts

Yield: 4 servings

*No brunch is complete without this dish.*

Combine the Chiken Breasts, broth powder, and water in a medium saucepan. Bring to a boil, cover, and simmer for 35 to 40 minutes or until tender.

While the Chiken Breasts are simmering, combine the mayonnaise, sour cream, lemon juice, lime juice, and sweetener in a medium bowl. Remove the Chiken Breasts from the broth, and chop into thin strips. Add the shredded Breasts, apples, celery, walnuts, and grapes to the mayonnaise mixture, and toss well.

4 textured soy Chiken Breasts

1 to 2 tablespoons vegetarian chicken-flavored broth powder or equivalent

3 cups water

¼ cup dairy-free mayonnaise

¼ cup soy sour cream

1 teaspoon lemon juice

1 teaspoon lime juice

1 tablespoon sweetener

1 cup chopped apples

¼ cup chopped celery

¼ cup chopped walnuts

¼ cup seedless green grape halves

Salads

Per Serving: Calories 202, Protein 12 g, Soy Protein 11 g, Fat 8 g, Carbohydrates 17 g, Sodium 287 mg

# Chiken Niçoise

*Yield: 4 servings*

*Try sprinkling vegetarian bacon bits on top of this.*

1 cup textured soy Chopped Chiken

1½ cups water

1 to 2 tablespoons vegetarian chicken-flavored broth powder or equivalent

5 new potatoes, cubed

½ pound fresh green beans

2 tablespoons red wine vinegar

1½ teaspoons Dijon mustard

1 teaspoon salt

½ teaspoon black pepper

6 tablespoons olive oil

¾ tablespoon minced fresh basil

1 tomato, sliced

1 cucumber, sliced

Combine the Chopped Chiken, water, and broth powder in a medium saucepan. Bring to a boil, cover, and simmer for 15 minutes or until tender.

In a medium saucepan, boil the potatoes until tender. In another medium saucepan, steam the green beans for 5 minutes or until tender.

In a small bowl, make a dressing by combining the red wine vinegar, mustard, salt, pepper, olive oil, and basil. In a large bowl, combine the cooked Chopped Chiken, potatoes, green beans, tomato, and cucumber. Pour the dressing over the salad, and toss.

Per Serving: Calories 410, Protein 13 g, Soy Protein 9 g, Fat 20 g, Carbohydrates 44 g, Sodium 766 mg

# Island Chiken Salad

*Yield: 4 servings*

*Use an apple if papaya is hard to find.*

Combine the chopped chiken, water, and broth powder in a medium saucepan. Bring to a boil, cover, and simmer for 15 minutes or until tender.

Make a dressing by combining the vinegar, oil, lime juice, sweetener, mustard, curry powder, salt, and pepper in a small bowl. Combine the bell peppers, papaya (or apple), onion, cilantro, and cooked Chopped Chiken in a mixing bowl. Toss with the dressing, chill for about 30 minutes, and serve.

1 cup textured soy Chopped Chiken

1½ cups water

1 to 2 tablespoons vegetarian chicken-flavored broth powder or equivalent

2 tablespoons white wine vinegar

⅓ cup olive oil

1 tablespoon lime juice

1 tablespoon sweetener

1½ teaspoons Dijon mustard

½ teaspoon curry powder

Salt and pepper, to taste

1 red bell pepper, chopped

1 green bell pepper, chopped

1 papaya, peeled and chopped

1 small red onion, chopped

1 tablespoon chopped fresh cilantro

Salads

Per Serving: Calories 268, Protein 10 g, Soy Protein 9 g, Fat 17 g, Carbohydrates 16 g, Sodium 221 mg

# Mandarin Chiken Salad

*Add chow mein noodles for a little extra crunch.*

⅓ cup chopped pecans

1 cup textured soy Chopped Chiken

1½ cups water

1 to 2 tablespoons vegetarian chicken-flavored broth powder or equivalent

⅓ cup olive oil

2 tablespoons red wine vinegar

One 11-ounce can Mandarin oranges, chilled and drained

2 green onions, chopped

¼ cup water chestnuts

1 bunch mixed greens

Salt and pepper, to taste

Preheat the oven to 350°F. Place the pecans on a baking sheet, and toast for 10 minutes. Combine the chopped chiken, water, and broth powder in a medium saucepan. Bring to a boil, cover, and simmer for 15 minutes or until tender.

Combine the oil and vinegar in small bowl. Combine the remaining ingredients, including the cooked Chopped Chiken, in a salad bowl. Toss the salad with the oil and vinegar mixture, and add salt and pepper to taste.

Salads

Per Serving: Calories 216, Protein 7 g, Soy Protein 6 g, Fat 14 g, Carbohydrates 13 g, Sodium 116 mg

# I Can't Believe
# It's Not Meat!

# Baked Goods
# & Sweets

# Crescent Pinwheels

*Yield: 8 servings*

*These are great served with pasta dishes or soups.*

½ cup water

½ cup beef-style textured soy protein granules

2 tablespoons soy Parmesan substitute

½ cup shredded soy mozzarella

1 teaspoon chopped fresh basil

¼ teaspoon ground pepper

½ teaspoon Cajun seasoning or Harvest Direct Sausage Seasoning, p. 8

2 tablespoons chopped green onions

4 oil-packed sun-dried tomatoes, drained and chopped

One 8-ounce can crescent rolls

In a small saucepan, bring the water to a boil. Add the textured soy granules, mix well, and let stand for 10 minutes.

Mix all the remaining ingredients, except for the crescent rolls. Add the granules to the mix, and combine thoroughly.

Preheat the oven to 375°F. Remove the crescent roll dough from the package, and keep in a rectangular shape. Press the cut dough seams together to seal. Spread the cheese and soy granule mixture on the dough, and roll up like a jelly roll along the long side. Cut into 1/4-inch slices, and place on oiled baking sheets. Bake for 15 minutes or until golden brown. Makes approximately 24 rolls.

Per Serving: Calories 256, Protein 9 g, Soy Protein 5 g, Fat 14 g, Carbohydrates 23 g, Sodium 504 mg

Baked Goods & Sweets

# High-Protein Granola

Yield: 12 servings

*Substitute any other nuts for the peanuts, if desired.*

In a large mixing bowl, combine all the ingredients, except the sweetener and oil, and mix thoroughly. In another bowl, combine the sweetener and oil. Mix well and add to the dry mixture. Combine thoroughly.

Preheat the oven to 275°F. Spread the granola evenly in a large, oiled baking dish so the mixture is about 1 to 2 inches thick. Bake for 15 minutes, then stir the mixture and return to the oven for about 20 minutes, or until the mixture begins to brown. Remove from the oven and let cool. Store in a tightly closed container.

2 cups rolled oats

½ cup unflavored textured soy protein granules

½ cup chopped slivered almonds

⅓ cup sunflower seeds

½ cup chopped unsalted peanuts

⅓ cup raisins

½ cup liquid sweetener

⅓ cup canola oil

Baked Goods
& Sweets

Per Serving: Calories 254, Protein 8 g, Soy Protein 2 g, Fat 14 g, Carbohydrates 28 g, Sodium 3 mg

# High-Protein Granola-Fruit Bars

*Yield: 48 bars*

*Substitute your favorite preserves for the prune mixture.*

2 cups dried pitted prunes

⅔ cup orange juice

½ cup chopped pecans

¾ cup dairy-free margarine

¾ cup packed brown sugar

¼ cup liquid sweetener

Egg replacer equivalent of 1 egg

1½ cups flour

1½ cups rolled oats

½ cup unflavored textured soy protein granules

1 teaspoon baking soda

Process the prunes with the orange juice in a blender until almost smooth, scraping down the sides of the blender a few times. Stir in the pecans and set the mixture aside.

In a large bowl, cream the margarine, brown sugar, and sweetener. Mix the egg substitute with the margarine mixture. Mix in the flour, oats, ¼ cup of the textured soy granules, and the baking soda, and blend thoroughly.

Preheat the oven to 325°F, and grease a 9 x 13-inch baking pan. Spread a little less than half of the flour and oatmeal mixture evenly in the pan. Then spread the prune and pecan mixture evenly over the flour mixture, keeping the prune mixture to within ½ inch of the edges of the pan. Crumble the remaining flour and oatmeal mixture over the top to cover the prune mixture, and sprinkle the top with the remaining textured soy granules. Press the top gently.

Bake for 30 to 35 minutes, or until the mixture has browned and springs back to the touch. Cool on a wire rack, and cut into 48 bars.

Per Serving: Calories 77, Protein 2 g, Soy Protein .5 g, Fat 2 g, Carbohydrates 14 g, Sodium 63 mg

Baked Goods & Sweets

# High-Protein Chocolate-Peanut Butter Fudge

*Yield: 24 bars*

*Satifsy the sweet tooth and still benefit from healthful soy.*

In a small saucepan, combine the corn syrup and brown sugar. Heat over medium-high heat until bubbly. Add the peanut butter and vanilla, and combine until well blended, then add the textured soy granules and mix well.

Remove from the heat and stir in the chocolate chips. Press into a greased 9 x 9-inch pan, and chill for 1 hour. Cut into 24 bars.

NOTE: Carob chips may be substituted for the chocolate chips.

½ cup light corn syrup

¼ cup light brown sugar

1½ cups peanut butter

1 tablespoon vanilla

¾ cup unflavored textured soy protein granules

1 cup semisweet dairy-free chocolate chips

Baked Goods & Sweets

Per Serving: Calories 162, Protein 6 g, Soy Protein 1 g, Fat 10 g, Carbohydrates 15 g, Sodium 87 mg

# Index

You can buy these vegetarian cookbooks at your local bookstore or natural foods store, or you may order directly from the publisher:

**Book Publishing Co.**
**P.O. Box 99**                    Please add $3.50 shipping per book
**Summertown, TN 38483**
**1-800-695-2241**

Tofu Cookery - $16.95

The TVP® Cookbook - $7.95

The New Farm Vegetarian Cookbook - $9.95

Meatless Burgers - $9.95

---

Many of the Harvest Direct textured soy products featured in this book are available at your local natural food store. If you cannot purchase them in your area, you may order them, as well as all the textured soy products in the recipes in this book, through:

**The Mail Order Catalog**
**P.O. Box 180**
**Summertown, TN 38483**
**1-800-695-2241**
**www.healthy-eating.com**